OF INSPIRATION:
Illustrations, Quotations, Poems and Selections

Speakers and Toastmasters Library, 0-8010-8327-3

1000 Tips and Quips for Speakers and Toastmasters,
Herbert V. Prochnow, 0-8010-6895-9

*A Treasury of Inspiration: Illustrations, Quotations, Poems,
and Selections,* Herbert V. Prochnow, 0-8010-6868-1

Stories for Speakers and Writers,
Erwin L. McDonald, 0-8010-5853-8

The Public Speaker's Handbook of Humor,
Helen and Larry Eisenberg, 0-8010-3278-4

A TREASURY
OF INSPIRATION:
Illustrations, Quotations,
Poems and Selections

by

HERBERT V. PROCHNOW

BAKER BOOK HOUSE
Grand Rapids, Michigan 49516

Previously published as
A Family Treasury of Inspiration and Faith

Fifth printing, October 1993

ISBN: 0-8010-6868-1

Library of Congress Catalog Card Number: 58-12417

Printed in the United States of America

PREFACE

Here is a treasury of inspiration and faith which it is hoped will be helpful to everyone in the family.

In life we sometimes face discouraging problems and even great hardships. Burdens frequently seem too heavy to carry, and we grow weary with the struggle. Sorrows and tragedies leave their heartaches and even their scars. Frustrations confuse and bewilder us. Goals which ambition led us so earnestly to seek are found to have little or no abiding value. Our pride, greed, vanity, jealousy, envy yield bitter fruits. Only a Christian faith adequately meets the recurring trials and problems of life.

In this volume there are approximately 400 items which have been selected for the wisdom and guidance they may give in meeting life's daily problems. There are inspiring illustrations, challenging selections from sermons by a number of ministers, great passages from the Bible, poems that touch the heart and significant quotations that strengthen faith.

This book need not be read at one time, but selections from it may be read from time to time for their inspiration and beauty.

Somehow we need to meet courageously life's hardest blows. We need the inward serenity and strength of a triumphant faith. We need also to lift our eyes unto the mountains with complete assurance that in the long way we must tread alone there is One who said, "Fear thou not, for I am with thee."

If this book helps in any way to give its readers a sense of this serenity and strength and assurance, it will have achieved a rewarding goal.

HERBERT V. PROCHNOW

GIVE US THE STRENGTH

Give us the strength to encounter that which is to come, that we may be brave in peril, constant in tribulation, temperate in wrath, and in all changes of fortune, and down to the gates of death, loyal and loving one to another.

Robert Louis Stevenson

PROGRESS

Every step of progress which the world has made has been from scaffold to scaffold, and from stake to stake.

Wendell Phillips

THE BIBLE

We search the world for truth; we cull the good,
the pure, the beautiful,
From all old flower fields of the soul;
And, weary seekers of the best,
We come back laden from our quest,
To find that all the sages said
Is in the Book our mothers read.

Whittier

FAME

But yesterday the word of Caesar might
Have stood against the world;
     now lies he there,
And none so poor to do him reverence.

Shakespeare

GREATNESS

He who comes up to his own idea of greatness, must always
have had a very low standard of it in his mind. *John Ruskin*

COURAGE AND SACRIFICE

One stormy day a coast guard was ordered to the rescue of a
liner wrecked off the coast of New England. An old and tried
seaman was in charge, but the members of the crew were for
the most part young, untested men. When one of them com-
prehended the situation, he turned white-faced to the captain
and said, "Sir, the wind is off-shore, the tide is running out.
We can go out, but against this wind and tide we cannot come
back."

The grim old captain faced the young man and said,
"Launch the boat; we go out."

"But, sir—" protested the young man.

"We don't have to come back," replied the captain.

WISDOM

No man ever got lost on a straight road. *Abraham Lincoln*

THOSE NOT SATISFIED

Blessed are they who are not satisfied to let well enough
alone. All the world is today we owe to them.

THANKSGIVING

I remember a preacher with very few of this world's goods, who had had sickness, leaving him sorely in debt. A destitute family knocked upon his door. He cared for them and sent them on their way with the last money that he had in his pocket. What he said when they left will ever be a lesson. "I thank God that you came to me so that I might have the privilege of being of some small help. Thank you so much for coming." It taught me a lesson. When people give you the privilege of helping them they are giving you the privilege of becoming like God and indeed you owe thanks to God for the opportunity.   *Ensworth Reisner*

MAKE MUCH OF IT

Children, look in those eyes, listen to that dear voice, notice the feeling of even a single touch that is bestowed upon you by that gentle hand! Make much of it while yet you have that most precious of all good gifts, a loving mother. Read the unfathomable love of those eyes; the kind anxiety of that tone and look, however slight your pain. In after life you may have friends, fond, dear friends, but never will you have again the inexpressible love and gentleness lavished upon you, which none but a mother bestows.   *Macaulay*

ONE THING MORE

I have now disposed of all my property to my family. There is one thing more I wish I could give them, and that is the Christian religion. If they had that, and I had not given them one shilling, they would have been rich, and if they had not that, and I had given them all the world, they would be poor.

Patrick Henry

WHAT MUST I DO TO BE SAVED

A refrain runs all through Acts: "What must I do to be saved?" . . . "Believe on the Lord Jesus Christ."

You must be clear at this point. There is nothing you can do to earn the forgiveness of God; no amount of "good works" will win His love . . . only your faith.

God is not impressed by your respectability. He is not flattered by your Sunday morning attention. He is not bribed by your deeds of charity.

Only one thing impresses God . . . *your faith.* All you can do—all you have to do—is to accept what He freely offers! Incredible, isn't it!

Of course, there's one hitch . . . faith means *commitment.* When you say, "I believe," you really say, "Here's my life; I haven't done so well; you had better take over."

You can't change yourself by dint of straining effort. But God can change you, if you give Him a fair chance . . . by giving him yourself.   *Chester A. Pennington*

FORGIVENESS

Humanity is never so beautiful as when praying for forgiveness, or else forgiving another.   *Richter*

FORGIVE AND FORGET

"I can forgive, but I cannot forget," is only another way of saying, "I will not forgive." Forgiveness ought to be like a cancelled note—torn in two, and burned up, so that it never can be shown against one.   *H. W. Beecher*

THE QUESTION

If you do believe in the Church of Jesus Christ and if you do believe in the good life, why don't you put them in first place instead of relegating them to a place of convenience? Why do so many of you in everyday life neglect the Church and things of the Spirit? "What shall it profit a man if he gain the whole world but lose his own soul?" This is finality. This is the Gospel. This is God's truth. In the final analysis, it is only the good life that counts. *C. Wesley Israel*

MEN OF GOD

General Omar Bradley said: "We have too many men of science; too few men of God. We have grasped the mystery of the atom and rejected the message of the Sermon on the Mount. Man is stumbling blindly through a spiritual darkness while toying with the precarious secrets of life and death. The world has achieved brilliance without wisdom, power without conscience. We know more about war than we know about peace, more about killing than we know about living." General Bradley is so right, and we all know it!

John Summerfield Wimbish

THE SABBATH

He that remembers not to keep the Christian Sabbath at the beginning of the week, will be in danger of forgetting, before the end of the week, that he is a Christian. *E. Turner*

WHAT IS THE HAPPIEST SEASON OF LIFE?

A wise old man, who had lived buoyantly through four score years, was asked, "Which is the happiest season of life?" He replied thoughtfully, "When spring comes, and in the soft air the buds are breaking on the trees, and they are covered with blossoms, I think, how beautiful is Spring! And when the summer comes, and covers the trees and bushes with heavy foliage, and singing birds mingle with the branches, I think, how beautiful is Summer! When autumn loads them with golden fruit, and their leaves bear the gorgeous tint of frost,

I think, how beautiful is Autumn! And when it is sore winter, and there is neither foliage nor fruit, then when I look up through the leafless branches and see, as I can see in no other season, the shining stars of heaven, I think, how beautiful is the Winter of life!"

CHARACTER

Good habits are not made on birthdays, nor Christian character at the New Year. The workshop of character is everyday life. The uneventful and commonplace hour is where the battle is lost or won.

LOOK AHEAD

Look not mournfully to the past—it comes not back again; wisely improve the present—it is thine; go forth to meet the shadowy future without fear, and with a manly heart.

Henry W. Longfellow

OLD AND NEW

We are continually told that we live in a "new" world. And it is true. Sometimes it is frightfully true! If people who died as little as fifty years ago were to come back to earth for a few days, they would be bewildered. The changes which have come about are humorously indicated with exaggeration in a little verse which appeared a short time ago. It is entitled "The Space Child's Mother Goose."

Mary had a little lamb,
Its fleece, electostatic.
And everywhere that Mary went
The lights became erratic.
It followed her to school one day,
Electrons all a jingle.
It made the children's hair rise up
And finger tips a tingle.
The teacher tried to turn it out

Her body was not grounded
The sparks were seen for miles away
And she's not yet rebounded.

This is a fantastic exaggeration, but it gives an idea, even though warped, of the strange new world about which even the children think.

But in the midst of so much that is new, there is the persistence of the old, the very old, in the world we inhabit. And the old things are more important in our lives than the new things.

An English minister put this truth memorably in describing a pastoral call which he recently made on a man who had lost a son. The minister said that he received the call over the telephone. The telephone was new, compared to what was known only a relatively short time ago. He took his automobile to go to the man's home. That was new. He went to the tall apartment house in which he lived. That was new. He rode up to the tenth floor in the elevator. That was new. Then he went in to face the man in his grief. That was not new. That was old. It was as old as King David, who sat in a room over a gate in Jerusalem and cried out over the death of his son: "Oh, Absalom, Absalom, my son, would God I had died for thee."

It is the old things that count most in our lives. Here, for instance, in every city is a person trying hard to keep his integrity of soul in the midst of temptations and pressures. That is not new. That is old. It is as old as Joseph in Egypt. Under temptation, he, too, struggled and cried: "Thou, God, seest me," and with God's help he preserved his soul from evil.

Our Christian faith brings these old things, the old reliance and helps, in the midst of this strange new world we have entered.

Here are some of the old things to which our gospel ministers. There is the old quest for God: "Oh, that I knew where

I might find him." Our gospel brings an answer to that search. It is found in the words of Philip in the first chapter of John: "We have found him." We can have the old, old assurance of trust in God: "The Lord is my shepherd." We can have the old gift of power: "I am strong for all things, in him who strengtheneth me."

From a sermon outline by Halford E. Luccock and Robert E. Luccock in Pulpit Digest

WHAT WILL IT MATTER

What matter will it be, O mortal man,
    when thou art dying,
Whether upon a throne or on the bare
    earth thou art lying?   *From the Persian*

NEVER LOSE

A kind deed is never lost, although you may not see its results.

NATURALNESS

How majestic is naturalness. I have never met a man whom I considered a great man who was not always natural and simple. Affectation is inevitably the mark of one not sure of himself.   *Charles G. Dawes*

MY DREAMS

Make my mortal dreams come true
With the work I fain would do:
Clothe with life the weak intent,
Let me be the thing I meant.

John Greenleaf Whittier

THE BEST PORTION

That best portion of a good man's life;
His little, nameless, unremembered acts
Of kindness and of love.   *Wordsworth*

CREATE IN ME A CLEAN HEART

Have mercy upon me, O God, according to thy loving kindness: according unto the multitude of thy tender mercies blot out my transgressions.

Wash me thoroughly from mine iniquity, and cleanse me from my sin.

For I acknowledge my transgressions: and my sin is ever before me . . .

Purge me with hyssop, and I shall be clean: wash me, and I shall be whiter than snow . . .

Create in me a clean heart, O God; and renew a right spirit within me.

Cast me not away from thy presence; and take not thy holy spirit from me.

Restore unto me the joy of thy salvation; and uphold me with thy free spirit.

Then will I teach transgressors thy ways; and sinners shall be converted unto thee.   *Psalm 51*

TWO LOVES

There are two loves from which all good and truth come: love of the Lord and love of the neighbor. And there are two loves from which all evils and falsities come: the love of self and the love of the world.   *Emanuel Swedenborg*

THOUGHTS

The way to destroy an enemy is to make him your friend.

The most promising young man is the one who does more than he promises.

Push others ahead, not aside.

We are not responsible for all the things that happen to us, but we are responsible for the way we behave when they do happen.

CHARITY

Though I speak with the tongues of men and of angels, and have not charity, I am become as sounding brass, or a tinkling cymbal . . .

And though I have the gift of prophecy, and understand all mysteries, and all knowledge; and though I have all faith, so that I could remove mountains, and have not charity, I am nothing . . .

And though I bestow all my goods to feed the poor, and though I give my body to be burned, and have not charity, it profiteth me nothing . . .

Charity suffereth long, and is kind; charity envieth not; charity vaunteth not itself, is not puffed up,

Doth not behave itself unseemly, seeketh not her own, is not easily provoked, thinketh no evil;

Rejoiceth not in iniquity, but rejoiceth in the truth;

Beareth all things, believeth all things, hopeth all things, endureth all things. . . .

And now abideth faith, hope, charity, these three; but the greatest of these is charity.   *13th Chapter of I Corinthians*

I BELIEVE IN THE LIFE EVERLASTING

According to our Christian revelation, God is our Father, His nature is goodness and love. A just and good Father does not create children, capable of growth and development, and full of growing aspiration, and then cast them into oblivion. He does not bid us to struggle for the development of character through long and hard years and then throw us aside. That would be like a sculptor who takes a piece of lovely marble and with infinite care begins to chisel the detail of a statue, continuing over long months or years; and then, having completed his masterpiece, takes a mallet and smashes it to bits. He would be insane. Neither will the Creator allow the process of character building to end in nothingness. Alfred Tennyson, the great English poet, struggled along with his doubt, occasioned by the death of his friend, Arthur Hallam, and came to this conclusion in the famous lines from "In Memoriam":

> Thou wilt not leave us in the dust;
> Thou madest man; he knows not why;—
> He thinks he was not made to die,
> And Thou hast made him; Thou art just!

A good God cares for His children. He does not put high hopes and aspirations into their hearts, only to fool them in the end. He does not bid us to struggle and strive for character development, only to bring us to frustration in the end. We are His children, and nothing can separate us from Him. As St. Paul said: "Neither life nor death, nor height nor depth or any other creature, can separate us from the love of God." Only so does life make sense. I believe in the life everlasting, because I believe in God.   *Robert C. Stanger*

DOING YOUR BEST

I do the best I know how, the very best I can; and I mean to keep on doing it to the end. If the end brings me out all right, what is said against me will not amount to anything. If the end brings me out all wrong, ten angels swearing I was right would make no difference.   *Abraham Lincoln*

GOOD WILL AMONG MEN

The world seems to be in quite a mess, but I can't fix it. I have the formula, but folks seem to be averse to using it.

It reads as follows: "Therefore all things whatsoever ye would that men should do to you, do ye even so unto them."

W. C. Thurston

PATIENCE

Charles Dickens, who later became one of the most famous and highest paid authors in the history of literature, got nothing for the first nine stories of his which were published. He received only five dollars for his tenth story.

LIBERTY

Liberty has never come from the government; it has always come from the subjects of it. The history of liberty is a history of limitation of governmental power, not the increase of it.

Woodrow Wilson

LIFE

We make a living by what we get, but we make a life by what we give.

Many men owe the grandeur of their lives to their tremendous difficulties.

Remember that what you possess in the world will be found at the day of your death to belong to another, but what you are will be yours forever.   *Henry van Dyke*

STRETCHING ONE'S SOUL

An impressive story was once told by R. Lee Sharpe of Carrollton, Ga., and published in the *Alabama Baptist*.

"I was just a kid," related Mr. Sharpe. "One spring day, father called me to go with him to old man Trussell's blacksmith shop. He had left a rake and a hoe to be repaired. And there they were ready, fixed like new. Father handed over a silver dollar for the repairing. But Mr. Trussell refused to take it. 'No,' he said, 'there's no charge for that little job.' But father insisted that he take the pay.

"If I live a thousand years," said Mr. Sharpe, "I'll never forget that great blacksmith's reply. 'Sid,' he said to my father, 'can't you let a man do something now and then—just to stretch his soul?'"

It is the old law. The giver receives a reward. Bread cast upon the waters comes back. One who "stretches his soul" into deeds of love and kindness, unfailingly reaps a just reward.

FAILURE

When Thomas Edison failed the first or second or third time in his attempts to discover something new, he did not mind it. He just kept on trying. It is said he made thousands upon thousands of trials before he got his celebrated electric light to operate. And this interesting story is told of him:

One day a workman, to whom he had given a task, came to him and said, "Mr. Edison, it cannot be done."

"How often have you tried?" asked Edison.

"About two thousand times," replied the man.

"Then go back and try it two thousand more times," said Edison. "You have only found out that there are two thousand ways in which it cannot be done."

THE MODESTY OF GEORGE WASHINGTON

The following quotation is from George Washington, at the time of his appointment as Commander-in-Chief of the United States:

"Tho' I am truly sensible of the high honor done me in this appointment yet I feel great distress from a consciousness that my abilities and military experience may not be equal to the extensive and important trust. However, as the Congress desire it, I will enter upon the momentous duty, and exert every power I possess in their service and for the support of the glorious cause. I beg they will accept my most cordial thanks for this distinguished testimony of their approbation.

"But lest some unlucky event should happen unfavorable to my reputation, I beg it may be remembered by every gentleman in the room that I this day declare, with the utmost sincerity, I do not think myself equal to the command I am honored with.

"As to pay, sir, I beg leave to assure the Congress that as no pecuniary consideration could have tempted me to accept this arduous employment at the expense of my domestic ease and happiness, I do not wish to make any profit from it. I will keep an exact account of my expenses. Those, I doubt not, they will discharge and that is all I desire."

ALL IN HIS POWER

Whatever woman may cast her lot with mine, should any ever do so, it is my intention to do all in my power to make her happy and contented; and there is nothing I can imagine that would make me more unhappy than to fail in the effort.

Abraham Lincoln: Letter to Mrs. O. H. Browning, April 1, 1838.

THE GENIUS OF WOMEN

God has placed the genius of women in their hearts; because the works of this genius are always works of love.

Lamartine

TO MEN ALONE

True love's the gift which God has given
To man alone beneath the heaven;
It is the secret sympathy,
The silver link, the silken tie,
Which heart to heart, and mind to mind,
In body and in soul can bind.

Sir Walter Scott, Lay of the Last Minstrel

BRING ME MEN

Bring me men to match my mountains;
  Bring me men to match my plains,—
Men with empires in their purpose,
  And new eras in their brains.

Sam Walter Foss

THERE ARE NO BARGAINS

The old Negro Spiritual proclaims "You can't go to Heaven in a rocking chair"; but that is the way most of us want to go. But we have nothing to offer except a Cross. There are no bargains. Religion is never cheap. There are no short cuts to the crown and avoiding the Cross. Jesus called to service, hardship and trial. Joy was to be found in acceptance, not avoidance. We have nothing to offer but religion with a Cross of sacrificial service for peace and joy.

Dr. Clinton C. Cox

DECISION

The Bible is a book of decision. Whether we read the Old Testament or the New Testament, it confronts men with the inescapable necessity to make up their minds. It unashamedly competes for men's minds. Such a Book of Decision fits squarely into our day and age. The Biblical theme is set there in the Book of Joshua: "Choose you this day whom you will serve; whether the gods which your fathers served or the gods of the Amorites. But as for me and my house, we will serve the Lord." That's decision.

Elijah puts the theme in all his derisive satire: "How long will you halt between two opinions? If the Lord be God, follow him; if Baal, then follow him. But the people answered not a word." That's indecision.

The Parable of the Prodigal has it: "And when he came

to himself, he said: 'I will arise and go to my father.'" That's decision.

Paul's preaching pronounces the theme as he stood in chains before Festus and Agrippa, and Agrippa said: "Paul, almost thou persuadest me to be a Christian." "Almost," "maybe," but not quite. That's indecision.

The Christian Faith demands of us something far more than Agrippa-like indecisions. It demands decision. The Bible says: God has done something for us; God has acted in Jesus Christ; the Lord God, Himself, was directly involved in the most cataclysmic, the most miraculous event in all history—the life and death and resurrection of Jesus Christ.

And you can't ignore God. This is mankind's great delusion—that God can be ignored if we choose. But you can't get away from God. We can no more ignore Him than we can ignore atomic power, or Russian Communism, or the sun in the heavens. We are His children. This is God's world. In this world He directly and unequivocably acted in the drama of human history, through Jesus Christ. Ignore Him? Indeed, life would be much more simple if we could, but we can't. The theme set by Joshua persists to this very moment and this very place but now that decision is personified in Christ: "Choose you this day whom you will serve." Amidst the battle for men's minds, to answer: "Almost thou persuadest me to be a Christian," is no sufficient answer. The Bible is a Book of Decision. Christian Faith demands decision. *From a sermon by George G. Parker*

AMBITION

Ambition has but one reward for all:
A little power, a little transient fame,
A grave to rest in, and a fading name!

William Winter

DOING IT TO HIS GLORY

In a village cemetery in England there is a monument with these simple words: "To Thomas Cobb, who mended shoes in this village for 40 years to the glory of God."

What a tribute to any man! We know little about Thomas Cobb otherwise, but this simple epitaph speaks volumes. His cobbler's bench was his altar before which he served . . .

It is one's high duty to make his occupation a vocation where he can serve to God's glory.

A poet says all this in simple but powerful verse for a housewife who serves before the sink in her kitchen. It might well speak for all of us, regardless of where we serve:

Lord of all, pots and pans and things . . .
Make me a saint by getting meals, and washing up the plates
Warm all the kitchen with Thy love, and light it with Thy
    Peace;
Forgive me all my worrying, and make all my grumbling
    cease.
Thou Who didst love to give men food, in room, or by the
    sea,
Accept this service that I do—I do unto Thee.

From a sermon by Paul L. Sturges

CHARACTER

Talent is nurtured in solitude; character is formed in the stormy billows of the world.   *Goethe*

    Not in the clamor of the crowded street,
    Not in the shouts and plaudits of the throng,
    But in ourselves, are triumph and defeat.

Longfellow

26

CHARITY

In men whom men condemn as ill
I find so much of goodness still,
In men whom men pronounce divine
I find so much of sin and blot
I do not dare to draw a line
Between the two, where God has not.

Joaquin Miller

Every charitable act is a stepping stone toward heaven.

Henry Ward Beecher

My poor are my best patients. God pays for them.

Boerhaave

Though I have all faith, so that I could remove mountains, and have not charity, I am nothing.   *I Corinthians XIII. 2*

And now abideth faith, hope, charity, these three; but the greatest of these is charity.   *I Corinthians XIII. 13*

As the purse is emptied the heart is filled.   *Victor Hugo*

I was an hungred, and ye gave me meat; I was thirsty, and ye gave me drink; I was a stranger, and ye took me in.

Matthew XXV. 35

FEAR NOT

Oh, fear not in a world like this,
and thou shalt know ere long,—
Know how sublime a thing it is
to suffer and be strong.

Henry Wadsworth Longfellow

IN MYSELF

I do not ask for any crown
  But that which all may win;
Nor try to conquer any world
  Except the one within.
Be thou my guide until I find
  Led by a tender hand,
The happy kingdom in myself
  And dare to take command!

Louisa May Alcott

KINDNESS

Be kind, for every one you meet is fighting a battle.

John Watson

I WONDER AS I WANDER

Back in the fall of 1933, an author was visiting the mountains of western North Carolina. Late one evening, he heard a mountain girl singing some hauntingly beautiful words. He asked her to sing them over for him while he jotted them down on a piece of paper. Later, the words were put to music and now the poem is fast becoming one of our best-loved Christmas carols:

I wonder as I wander out under the sky,
How Jesus our Saviour did come forth to die,
For poor ornery people like you and like I,
I wonder as I wander, out under the sky.

This simple, plaintive setting expresses some of the things we do wonder about. How the Almighty God, Who is from ever-lasting to ever-lasting could come down to this earth in the person of a little Babe at Bethlehem is a mystery that only faith can even begin to understand.

Dr. John S. Wimbish

BREAD

Cast thy bread upon the waters: for thou shalt find it after many days.   *Ecclesiastes XI. 1*

What man is there of you, whom if his son ask bread, will he give him a stone?   *Matthew VII. 9*

Jesus said unto them, I am the bread of life: he that cometh to me shall never hunger; and he that believeth on me shall never thirst.   *John VI. 35*

THE RECORD OF HISTORY

The sages and heroes of history are receding from us, and history contracts the record of their deeds into a narrower and narrower page. But time has no power over the name and deeds and words of Jesus Christ.   *Channing*

Alexander, Caesar, Charlemagne and I myself have founded empires; but upon what do these creations of our genius depend? Upon force. Jesus alone founded His empire upon love; and to this very day millions would die for Him.

Napoleon

CHRISTIANITY AND ITS DOCTRINE

Christianity, with its doctrine of humility, of foregiveness, of love, is incompatible with the state, with its haughtiness, its violence, its punishment, its wars.   *Tolstoy*

CHRISTMAS

O little town of Bethlehem,
  How still we see thee lie!
Above thy deep and dreamless sleep
  The silent stars go by.   *Phillips Brooks*

I heard the bells on Christmas Day
Their old, familiar carols play,
And wild and sweet
The words repeat
Of peace on earth, good-will to men!

Longfellow

For unto you is born this day in the city of David, a
Saviour, which is Christ the Lord.   *Luke II. 11*

God rest ye, little children;
      let nothing you affright,
For Jesus Christ, your Saviour,
      was born this happy night;
Along the hills of Galilee the
      white flocks sleeping lay,
When Christ, the Child of
      Nazareth, was born on
      Christmas Day.   *Dinah Mulock Craik*

Hark the herald angels sing,
"Glory to the new-born king."
Peace on earth, and mercy mild,
God and sinners reconciled!

Charles Wesley

A GREAT WORLD

I never weary of great churches. It is my favourite kind of
mountain scenery. Mankind was never so happily inspired
as when it made a cathedral.   *Stevenson*

DEATH

Man that is born of a woman hath but a short time to live, and is full of misery. He cometh up, and is cut down, like a flower; he fleeth as it were a shadow, and never continueth in one stay. *Book of Common Prayer*

DEATH

Death lies on her, like an untimely frost
Upon the sweetest flower of all the field.

Shakespeare

First our pleasures die—and then our hopes,
and then our fears—and when
These are dead, the debt is due,
Dust claims dust—and we die too. *Shelley*

EASTER

Tomb, thou shalt not hold
      Him longer;
Death is strong, but Life is
      stronger;
Stronger than the dark, the
      light;
Stronger than the wrong, the
      right;
Faith and Hope triumphant
      say
Christ will rise on Easter Day.

Phillips Brooks

FAME

A tomb now suffices him for whom the whole world was not sufficient. *Epitaph on Alexander the Great*

THE CULT OF EASY RELIGION

We live under the influence of the cult of easy religion. One cannot pick up a Sunday supplement without finding words of encouragement and advice for happy and poised living. Stand in front of any newsstand and you will count, as I did in Boston, over 29 magazines out of a total of some 72 that tell you how to live the happy life. I know something of the heartbreak and the unrest of people in a great city. We all desperately need whatever aids we can find that will enable us to live the happy life, but there is in these books and lessons on easy religion, something which makes me tremble and fear. God is pictured very much as a glorified bell-captain. He is always there on the edge of your life. If you beckon, He comes. If you don't crook your fingers, He stays at a respectful distance. If you are in trouble and you need a lift with the baggage of life, He's there to pick it up and carry it for you. This to me is a far cry from the God of the New Testament. Nowhere in any of these booklets or magazines will you find anything that suggests that you are a sinner. You are frustrated; you may have a divided personality; you may live under awful handicaps and tremendous limitations; but in prosperous America it's hard to find a sinner—a sinner under the judgment of God, the kind of judgment the New Testament says will separate the sheep from the goats. We would like to forget that the New Testament speaks of a God who says, even though His heart is broken, "Depart from me for I never knew you." I haven't read a page in any of these books on easy religion that suggests that any of us should say as Peter said, "Lord depart from me for I am a sinful man." (Luke 5:8) No, God is there. He won't intrude. If you beckon, He comes and all that He ever desires to do for you is to give you perpetual peace and prosperity as your present possession. Any minister is grateful for anything or anyone who helps someone to live

for Christ, but Paul in this same letter to Timothy warned
against false teachings and unwise sayings. This cult of easy
religion needs to be examined in the light of the New Testament. *Dr. Robert J. Lamont*

ATONEMENT

We love the doctrine of the Atonement—the teaching that
Jesus Christ shed his precious blood as the remission for our
sins. We all want to go to heaven, just like some of us would
like to go to New England or Florida. We think the climate
is good there and we have friends we would like to see, but
somehow that Cross on which Christ died, though it is 2000
years old, is still a very modern challenge. You cannot go and
kneel at the foot of the Cross and confess your sins and receive the grace of Christ there, without also rising as you leave
and hearing the One who died say, "If any man will come
after me, let him take his cross daily and follow me." (Luke
9:23) Now you can thrust your conscience aside and so-doing
makes it easy to thrust aside also the daily Cross which marks
us as children of our Heavenly Father, but let that conscience
speak and have its way, then that Cross, stained with blood so
divine, becomes identified in all our living.

Dr. Robert J. Lamont

HIS OBJECTIVE

I desire so to conduct the affairs of this administration that
if at the end, when I come to lay down the reins of power,
I have lost every other friend on earth, I shall at least have one
friend left, and that friend shall be down inside of me.

Lincoln

HOLY GROUND

Ay, call it holy ground,
The soil where first they trod,

They have left unstained,
    what there they found—
Freedom to worship God.

    Felicia D. Hemans—The Landing of the
    Pilgrim Fathers

THOUGHTS

The biggest mistake is the fear that you will make one.

Only a comparative few recognize opportunity, because it is disguised as hard work.

REVENGE

When a man does not retaliate when injured, he wraps around him the royal robes of calmness, and goes quietly on his way.

KINDNESS

Not only to say the right thing in the right place, but far more difficult, to leave unsaid the wrong thing at the tempting moment.

GOD

God moves in a mysterious way
His wonders to perform;
He plants his footsteps in the sea
And rides upon the storm.   *Cowper*

A mighty fortress is our God,
A bulwark never failing,
Our helper he amid the flood
Of mortal ills prevailing.   *Luther*

God is our refuge and strength, a very present help in trouble.   *Psalms XLVI. 1*

IMMORTALITY

A good man never dies.   *Callimachus*

Then shall the dust return to the earth as it was; and the spirit shall return unto God who gave it.

Ecclesiastes XII. 7

Oh, may I join the choir invisible
Of those immortal dead who live again.

George Eliot

Life is the childhood of our immortality.   *Goethe*

There is no death! the stars go down to rise upon some fairer shore.   *J. L. McCreery*

The nearer I approach the end, the plainer I hear around me the immortal symphonies of the worlds which invite me. It is marvelous, yet simple.   *Victor Hugo*

For tho' from out our bourne of time and place
The flood may bear me far,
I hope to see my Pilot face to face
When I have crost the bar.   *Tennyson*

PASS IT ON

Have you had a kindness shown?
Pass it on;
'Twas not given for thee alone,
Pass it on;
Let it travel down the years,
Let it wipe another's tears,
'Til in Heaven the deed appears—
Pass it on.   *Rev. Henry Burton*

HE WHO KNOWS
He who knows others is learned;
He who knows himself is wise.   *Lao-Tsze*

IS IT ONLY A FAIRY TALE?
Every man's life is a fairy-tale written by God's fingers.
Hans Christian Andersen

ONLY ONCE
I expect to pass through this world but once. Any good therefore that I can do, or any kindness that I can show to any fellow creature, let me do it now. Let me not defer or neglect it, for I shall not pass this way again.

IGNOBLE EASE
I wish to preach not the doctrine of ignoble ease, but the doctrine of the strenuous life.   *Theodore Roosevelt*

FAR FROM HOME
Lead, kindly Light, amid the encircling gloom,
Lead Thou me on!
The night is dark, and I am far from home—
Lead Thou me on!
Keep Thou my feet; I do not ask to see
The distant scene,—one step enough for me.
John Henry Newman

MAN IS IMMORTAL
I decline to accept the end of men . . . I believe that man will not merely endure; he will prevail. He is immortal not because he alone among creatures has an inexhaustible voice but because he has a soul, a spirit capable of compassion and sacrifice and endurance.

William Faulkner—Acceptance Speech for Nobel Prize in Literature, 1949.

KNOW THYSELF

Know then thyself, presume not God to scan;
The proper study of mankind is man.

Pope—Essay on Man

MONUMENTS

Monuments! what are they? the very pyramids have forgotten their builders, or to whom they were dedicated. Deeds, not stones, are the true monuments of the great.   *Motley*

DEATHLESS LOVE

There is none,
In all this cold and hollow
    world, no fount
Of deep strong, deathless love,
    save that within
A mother's heart.   *Felicia D. Hemans*

A GOOD NAME

Good name in man and woman, dear my lord,
Is the immediate jewel of their souls;
Who steals my purse steals trash; 'tis something, nothing;
'Twas mine, 'tis his, and has been slave to thousands;
But he that filches from me my good name
Robes me of that which not enriches him,
And makes me poor indeed.   *Shakespeare*

HE LEADETH ME

He Leadeth Me—
In pastures green? No, not always,
Sometimes He who knowest best,
In kindness leadeth me in weary ways
Where heavy shadows be;
Out of the sunshine warm and soft and bright,

Out of the sunshine into the darkest night,
I oft would yield to sorrow and to fright,
Only for this: I know He holds my hand.
So, whether led in green or desert land.
I trust, although I cannot understand.

He leadeth me—
Beside still waters? No, not always so.
Oft times the heavy tempests round me blow,
And o'er my soul the waves and billows go,
But when the storm beats wildest, and I cry
Aloud for help, the Master standeth by
And whispers to my soul: "Lo, it is I."
Above the tempest wild I hear Him say:
"Beyond the darkness lies the perfect day;
In every path of thine I lead the way."

So whether on the hilltops, high and fair
I dwell, or in the sunless valleys, where
The shadows lie—what matter? He is there.
And more than this. Where'er the pathway lead
He gives me no helpless, broken reed,
But His own hand, sufficient for my need.
So where He leads me I can safely go.
And in the blest hereafter I shall know
Why in His wisdom He hath led me so.

*From Tom M. Olson's page in LeTourneay Tech's
Now. (As reprinted in Sunshine Magazine)*

AGE

As a white candle in a holy place,
So is the beauty of an aged face.

Joseph Campbell

AMERICA

Bring to me men to match my mountains,
Bring me men to match my plains,
Men with empires in their purpose,
And new eras in their brains.   *S. W. Foss*

THE BEAUTY TO BE

Lord of the far horizons,
Give us the eyes to see
Over the verge of the sundown
The beauty that is to be.

Bliss Carman, Lord of the Far Horizons

EXPERIENCE SHOWS

Knowing, what all experience serves to show,
No mud can soil us but the mud we throw.

James Russell Lowell

A CHANCE

My country owes me nothing. It gave me, as it gives to
every boy and girl, a chance. It gave me schooling, independence of action, opportunity for service and honor. In no other
land could a boy from a country village, without inheritance
or influential friends, look forward with unbounded hope.

Herbert Hoover

IN OURSELVES

Not in the clamor of the crowded street,
  Not in the shouts and plaudits of the throng,
But in ourselves are triumph and defeat.

Henry Wadsworth Longfellow

HELP LIVE

It isn't enough to believe in the philosophy of live and let live. You have to believe in the greater idea of live and help live.

SUCCESS

Some persons think they have made a success of life when all they have made is money.

THY DUTY

Do thy duty; that is best;
Leave unto thy Lord the rest.

James Russell Lowell

THE TEST OF GOOD WORKS

What does it profit, if a man says he has faith, but has not works? Can his faith save him? If a brother or sister is ill-clad and in lack of daily food, and one of you says to them, "Go in peace, be warmed and filled," without giving them the things needed for the body, what does it profit? So, faith by itself, if it has not works, is dead.

But someone will say, "You have faith, and I have works." Show me your faith apart from your works, and I, by my works, will show you my faith. For as the body apart from the spirit is dead, so faith apart from works is dead.

The words of Apostle James, 2d Letter

THE RICH FOOL

And he told them a parable, saying: The land of a rich man brought forth plentifully, and he thought to himself, "What shall I do, for I have nowhere to store my crops?" And he said, "I will do this: I will pull down my barns, and build larger ones; and there I will store all my grain and my goods. And I will say to my soul, 'Soul, you have ample goods laid

up for many years; take your ease, eat, drink, be merry.'"
But God said to him, "Fool! This night your soul is required of you, and the things you have prepared, whose will they be?"
So is he who lays up treasure for himself, and is not rich toward God. *St. Luke's Gospel, 12th Chapter*

MEMORY

Across the fields of yesterday
  He sometimes comes to me,
A little lad just back from play—
  The lad I used to be.

T. S. Jones, Jr., Sometimes

A CHILDISH IGNORANCE

I remember, I remember
The fir-trees dark and high;
I used to think their slender tops
Were close against the sky:
It was a childish ignorance,
But now 'tis little joy
To know I'm farther off from heav'n
Than when I was a boy.   *Thomas Hood*

CHARITY

Though I speak with the tongues of men and of angels, and have not charity, I am become as sounding brass or a tinkling cymbal.   *New Testament, I Corinthians XIII*

And now abideth faith, hope, charity, these three; but the greatest of these is charity.   *New Testament, I*
New Testament, I Corinthians, XIII, 13

Verily I say unto you, Inasmuch as ye have done it unto one of the least of these my brethren, ye have done it unto me.   *New Testament, Matthew, XXV, 40*

A GREEN HILL

There is a green hill far away,
  Without a city wall,
Where the dear Lord was crucified,
  Who died to save us all.

Cecil Frances Alexander

AGE AND ACCOMPLISHMENT

Since when has age become a disqualifying factor in human endeavor and accomplishments? Between the ages of 70 and 83, Commodore Vanderbilt added ten million dollars to his fortune. Verdi, at 83, produced his magnificent "Te Deum," his "Stabat Mater," and "Ave Maria."

Oliver Wendell Holmes, at 79, wrote his "Over the Tea-cups," and Tennyson, at 83, wrote "Crossing the Bar."

CONSCIENCE

Conscience is God's presence in man.   *Swedenborg*

THE SECRET OF PEACE

"You have heard that it is said, 'An eye for an eye and a tooth for a tooth.' But I say to you, do not resist one who is evil. But if anyone strikes you on the right cheek, turn to him the other also and if anyone would sue you, and take your coat, let him have your cloak also; and if anyone forces you to go one mile, go with him two miles. Give to him who begs from you, and do not refuse him who would borrow from you."

"You have heard it said, 'You shall love your neighbor and hate your enemy.' But I say to you, love your enemy, and pray for those who persecute you, so that you may be sons of your Father who is in heaven; for he makes his sun to rise on the evil and on the good, and sends rain on the just and on the unjust." *Jesus, in St. Matthew 5.*

DEATH

Sunset and evening star,
  And one clear call for me!
And may there be no moaning of the bar
  When I put out to sea

.   .   .   .

I hope to see my Pilot face to face
  When I have crost the bar.

WHEN WE PLAY THE FOOL

But when we play the fool, how wide
The theatre expands! beside,
How long the audience sits before us!
How many prompters! what a chorus!

Landor

A MIGHTY FORTRESS

A mighty fortress is our God,
  A bulwark never failing.

Martin Luther

WHO IS YOUR NEIGHBOR?

But he, trying to justify himself, said to Jesus, "And who is my neighbor?"

Jesus replied, "A man was going down from Jerusalem to Jericho, and he fell among robbers, who stripped him and beat him, and departed leaving him half dead.

"Now, by chance, a priest was going down that road, and when he saw him, he passed by on the other side. So, likewise, a Levite, when he came to the place and saw him, passed by on the other side.

"But a Samaritan, as he journeyed, came to where he was, and when he saw him, he had compassion, and went to him and bound up his wounds, pouring on oil and wine. Then he set him on his own beast and brought him to an inn, and took care of him. And the next day he took out two denarii, and gave them to the innkeeper, saying, 'Take care of him; and whatever more you spend, I will repay you when I come back.'

"Which of these three, do you think, proved neighbor to the man who fell among the robbers?"

He said, "The man who showed mercy on him."

And Jesus said to him, "Go and do likewise."

St. Luke, 10

THE INEVITABLE HOUR

The boast of heraldry, the pomp of pow'r.
    And all that beauty, all that wealth e'er gave,
Awaits alike th' inevitable hour,
    The paths of glory lead but to the grave.   *Gray*

OUR ETERNAL HOME

O God, our help in ages past,
    Our hope for years to come,
Our shelter from the stormy blast,
    And our eternal home.   *Isaac Watts*

IMMORTALITY

Fool! All that is, at all,
Lasts ever past recall;
Earth changes, but thy soul and God stand sure;
What entered into thee,
That was, is, and shall be:
Time's wheel runs back or stops; Potter and clay endure.

R. Browning

44

ONLY GOD

For a cup and bells our loves we pay,
  Bubbles we buy with a whole soul's tasking:
'Tis *heaven* alone that is given away,
  'Tis only God may be had for the asking.

J. R. Lowell

WHERE ARE THE NINE?

On the way to Jerusalem, he was passing along between Samaria and Galilee. And as he entered a village, he was met by ten lepers, who stood at a distance and lifted up their voices, and said, "Jesus, Master, have mercy on us!"

When he saw them, he said to them, "Go and show yourselves to the priests."

And as they went, they were cleansed. Then one of them, when he saw that he was healed, turned back, praising God with a loud voice. And he fell on his face at Jesus' feet, giving him thanks.

Now, he was a Samaritan.

Then Jesus said, "Were not ten cleansed? Where are the nine? Was no one found to return and give praise to God except this foreigner?" And he said to him, "Rise and go your way; your faith has made you well."   *St. Luke, 17*

BEYOND THESE TEARS

Beyond this vale of tears
  There is a life above,
Unmeasured by the flight of years;
  And all that life is love.

James Montgomery

THIS LIFE

This life is but the passage of a day,
This life is but a pang and all is over;
But in the life to come which fades not away
Every love shall abide and every lover.

Christina Rossetti

FOR WHOM THE BELL TOLLS

. . . any man's death diminishes me, because I am involved
in Mankinde; and therefore never send to know for whom
the bell tolls; It tolls for thee.   *John Donne*

SCARS

God will not look you over for medals, degrees or diplomas,
but for scars.   *Elbert Hubbard*

KINDNESS

'Twas a thief said the last kind word to Christ;
Christ took the kindness, and forgave the theft.

R. Browning

LIFE

A crust of bread and a corner to sleep in,
A minute to smile and an hour to weep in,
A pint of joy to a peck of trouble,
And never a laugh but the moans come double;
    And that is life!   *Paul Laurence Dunbar*

Like leaves on trees the race of man is found,
Now green in youth, now with'ring on the ground:
Another race the following spring supplies,
They fall successive and successive rise.   *Homer*

CONVERSION

How encouraging it would be to believe that all who accept church membership through the regular channels of Christian education and worship would endure unto the end! Many who once were numbered among us here in First Church "went out because they were not of us." For reasons known only to God and to themselves, many so-called Christians fall away.

Dwight L. Moody took occasion to tell the story of a meeting between himself and a man who tottered along obviously under the influence of alcohol. "Oh, it's you, is it Mr. Moody?" asked the intoxicated man. "Don't you know me? I am one of your converts." Moody put an arm around the man to steady him and said, "Well, my son, you look like one of mine— you're surely not one of the Lord's."

Like it or not, we must honestly and seriously look at "this experience called conversion." It is Jesus Christ who forces the issue upon us. Jesus said, "Except ye be converted, and become as little children, ye shall not enter into the kingdom of heaven." (Matthew 18:3) Not Paul nor John nor Peter, but it is Jesus Himself who makes conversion the only entrance into the Kingdom of God. . . .

Arthur Koestler in his autobiography speaks of his conversion back from Communism to western democractic idealism. He had completely revamped his thinking and redirected his purposes. Now, when you use the word conversion in Christianity, you are not speaking of winning people to a new system of ethics or to a new concept of philosophy, or even to a new pattern of doctrine. You are talking about people coming from the experience of serving themselves to the place of such total submission to Jesus Christ that they are converted to a Person. It is true that from that Person, a philosophy will come and it is true that out of that philosophy will come a system of ethics. You are not, however, a Christian because you embrace a position in doctrine or because you hold to an essentially religious attitude in ethical concern. You are only a Christian when you know in your heart, as I know in mine, that out of our need in sin, we have submitted ourselves to Jesus Christ in such utter dependence upon His death on the Cross for us, that we rise up new men and new women, quickened from death into life.   *Dr. Robert J. Lamant*

LIFE

Tomorrow will I live, the fool does say;
Today itself's too late; the wise lived yesterday.

Martial.

As for man his days are as grass; as a flower of the field, so he flourisheth.

The wind passeth over it, and it is gone; and the place thereof shall know it no more.   *Psalms, CIII, 15, 16.*

MONEY

Money may be the husk of many things, but not the kernel. It brings you food, but not appetite; medicine, but not health, acquaintance, but not friends; servants, but not loyalty; days of joy, but not peace or happiness.   *Henrik Ibsen*

CHILDREN'S BILL OF RIGHTS

1. The right to the affection and intelligent guidance of understanding parents.
2. The right to be raised in a decent home in which he or she is adequately fed, clothed, and sheltered.
3. The right to the benefits of religious guidance and training.
4. The right to a school program, which, in addition to sound academic training, offers maximum opportunity for individual development and preparation for living.

48

5. The right to receive constructive discipline for the proper development of good character, conduct and habits.

6. The right to be secure in his or her community against all influences detrimental to wholesome development.

7. The right to the individual selection of free and wholesome recreation.

8. The right to live in a community in which adults practice the belief that the welfare of their children is of primary importance.

9. The right to receive good adult example.

New York Youth Commission

ONLY THOSE

Only those are crowned and sainted
Who with grief have been acquainted.

Henry Wadsworth Longfellow

DO YOU HAVE CHARACTER?

It takes character to keep from talking about others when others around you are talking; to stand up for an absent person who is being abused; to be somebody by holding fast to your ideals when it causes you to be looked upon as queer; to refuse to do a thing that is wrong, though others do it— but that is what makes character.

WE HAVE NEED

We all have need of that prayer of the British mariner: "Save us, O God, Thine ocean is so large, and our little boat so small." *Canon Farrar*

LOVE

Talk not of wasted affection, affection never was wasted;
If it enrich not the heart of another, its waters, returning
Back to their springs, like the rain, shall fill them full of
refreshment. *Henry Wadsworth Longfellow*

IT IS NOT A SLIGHT THING

I love little children, and it is not a slight thing when they, who are fresh from God, love us.   *Dickens*

YOU CAN HELP

There is hardly a man who would not struggle to come back if he felt that someone believed in him; believed that he could do it.

A MILE AND A HALF FROM CHURCH

We're a mile and a half from church, you know, and it rains today, so we can't go. We'd go ten miles to a party or show, though the rains should fall and the winds should blow. That's why, when it rains, we just can't go. But we always go to the things we like, and we ride if we can; if we can't, we hike.

We're a mile and a half from church, you know, and a tire is flat, so we can't go. We'd fix it twice to make a visit, and if there's a ball game we wouldn't miss it. We'd mend the tire if at all we could, and if we couldn't, we'd go afoot, for hunting pleasure is all the style, so the church will have to wait awhile.

We're a mile and a half from church, you know, and our friends are coming, so we can't go. To disappoint our friends would seem unkind, but to neglect worship we don't mind, if we may please our friends on earth, and spend a day in feasting and mirth. But, sometime, when we come near the end of our days, we'll go to church and mend our ways.

George C. Degen

WHAT IS RIGHT?

It is not who is right that is of greatest importance, but what is right.

THE LORD WAS THEIR SHEPHERD

The first thing they did when they got off the ship was to kneel down under the open sky and thank God. That was why they had come here—to meet God in the way they thought right. It was a simple, manly way they had with Him. Each man seeking His presence, reading His Word, listening to His voice, trying to understand His way and to live it. Each man a free man, responsible to God.

It was not only on Sundays, or in church alone, that they thought of Him, but always and everywhere. They felt that the world was God's house, and they walked reverently in it, and they tried to remember to live by His ways.

So it was that when they wrote a Declaration of Independence, in that fateful moment of making themselves a nation, they called upon Him to behold the justice of what they were about to do. And when they met to draw up a Constitution, governing how Americans should behave toward each other, they sank to their knees and prayed for guidance from the Highest Lawgiver of all.

And from that day to this, when we come together to make a solemn public decision, we take a moment to ask God to make our minds wise, and our hearts good, and our motives pure.

Surely there never was a better country to find God in. Out on the open coast, where the ocean stirs forever and ever, always changing and always the same; on the prairies where the grass blows, and ripens, and dies, and is born again; in the wild, high mountains, and in the silent desert—everywhere under this wide sky the feeling comes: Some one has been here. Some one has made this beautiful for me. Some one expects me to be worthy of this!

Some one expects me to be worthy! Through most of our history we have lived with that faith. And only as long as we believe it, and go on living it, will we be secure.

*From an advertisement of the John Hancock
Mutual Life Insurance Company of Boston*

THE LORD IS GOOD

Make a joyful noise unto the Lord, all ye lands.
Serve the Lord with gladness:
Come before his presence with singing.
Know ye that the Lord he is God: it is he that hath made us,
    and not we ourselves;
We are his people, and the sheep of his pasture.
Enter into his gates with thanksgiving, and into his courts
    with praise:
Be thankful unto him, and bless his name.
For the Lord is good; his mercy is everylasting;
And his truth endureth to all generations.   *Psalm 100*

THIS IS A FAITHFUL SAYING

This is a faithful saying, and worthy of all acceptation, that
Christ Jesus came into the world to save sinners; of whom
I am chief. Howbeit for this cause I obtained mercy, that in
me first Jesus Christ might show forth all long-suffering, for
a pattern to them which should hereafter believe in him to
life everlasting. Now unto the King eternal, immortal, invisible, the only wise God, be honor and glory for ever and
ever. Amen.   *I Timothy 1:15-17*

PAIN

Pain is hard to bear . . .
But with patience, day by day
Even this shall pass away.

Theodore Tilton

LEAVE THE VISION CLEAR

Thank God, bless God, all ye who suffer not
More grief than he can weep for; . . . for tears will run
Soon in long rivers down the lifted face,
And leave the vision clear for stars and sun.

Elizabeth Barrett Browning

HE HATH SHOWED THEE

He hath showed thee, O man, what is good; and what doth
the Lord require of thee, but to do justly, and to love mercy,
and to walk humbly with thy God?   *Micah 6:8*

FAITH

The Lord is my shepherd;
I shall not want.
He maketh me to lie down in green pastures:
He leadeth me beside the still waters.
He restoreth my soul:
He leadeth me in the paths of righteousness for his name's
     sake.
Yea, though I walk through the valley of the shadow of death,
     I will fear no evil:
For thou art with me; thy rod and thy staff they comfort me.
Thou preparest a table before me in the presence of mine
     enemies:
Thou anointest my head with oil; my cup runneth over.
Surely goodness and mercy shall follow me all the days of
     my life:
And I will dwell in the house of the Lord for ever.

Psalm 23

COMFORT

There are wounds of the spirit which never close, and are
intended in God's mercy to bring us nearer to Him, and to

prevent us leaving Him, by their very perpetuity. Such wounds, then, may almost be taken as a pledge, or at least as a ground for the humble trust, that God will give us the great gift of perseverance to the end. . . . This is how I comfort myself in my own great bereavements.   *John Henry Newman*

TO LIVE

To live in hearts we leave behind
Is not to die.   *Thomas Campbell*

THE BEGGAR AND THE KING

Sooner or later, all things pass away,
And are no more: The beggar and the king,
With equal steps, tread forward to their end.

Thomas Southerne

ANGEL OF PATIENCE

To weary hearts, to mourning homes,
God's meekest Angel gently comes:
No power has he to banish pain,
Or give us back our lost again;
And yet in tenderest love, our dear
And Heavenly Father sends him here.

There's quiet in that Angel's glance,
There's rest in his still countenance!
He mocks no grief with idle cheer,
Nor wounds with words the mourner's ear;
But ills and woes he may not cure
He kindly trains us to endure.

Angel of Patience! sent to calm
Our feverish brows with cooling palm;
To lay the storms of hope and fear,
And reconcile life's smile and tear;

The throbs of wounded pride to still,
And make our own our Father's will!

O thou who mournest on thy way,
With longings for the close of day;
He walks with thee, that Angel kind,
And gently whispers, "Be resigned;
Bear up, bear on, the end shall tell
The dear Lord ordereth all things well!"

John Greenleaf Whittier

HOPE

Hope, child, tomorrow, and tomorrow still,
  And every morrow hope; trust while you live,
Hope! each time the dawn doth heaven fill,
  Be there to ask as God is there to give.

Victor Hugo

BETTER BEGIN NOW

A young girl said to her mother, just after a white-haired visitor had left their home, "If I could be such a nice old lady as that—so beautiful and sweet—I wouldn't mind growing old."

The mother replied, "Well, Janie, if you want to be that kind of an old lady, you'd better begin now. She didn't become a lady like that in a hurry."

A VICE

The foolish and wicked practice of cursing and swearing is a vice so mean and low that everyone of sense and character detests and despises it.   *George Washington*

I KNOW

Yet, in the maddening maze of things,
And tossed by storm and flood,
To one fixed trust my spirit clings:
I know that God is good!

John Greenleaf Whittier

BE NOT TROUBLED

Peace I leave with you, my peace I give unto you: not as the
world giveth, give I unto you. Let not your heart be troubled,
neither let it be afraid. *John 14:27*

WHOM SHALL I FEAR

The Lord is my light and my salvation; whom shall I fear?
The Lord is the strength of my life; of whom shall I be afraid?

Psalm 27:1

AM I NOT RICHER

And yet, dear heart! remembering thee,
Am I not richer than of old?
Safe in thy immortality,
What change can reach the wealth I hold?
What chance can mar the pearl and gold
Thy love hath left in trust for me?
And while in life's long afternoon,
Where cool and long the shadows grow,
I walk to meet the night that soon
Shall shape and shadow overflow,
I cannot feel that thou art far,
Since near at need the angels are;
And when the sunset gates unbar,
Shall I not see thee waiting stand,

And, white against the evening star,
The welcome of thy beckoning hand?

From "Snow-bound" by John Greenleaf Whittier

THE RAINY DAY

The day is cold, and dark, and dreary;
It rains, and the wind is never weary;
The vine still clings to the mouldering wall,
But at every gust the dead leaves fall,
    And the day is dark and dreary.

My life is cold, and dark, and dreary;
It rains, and the wind is never weary;
My thoughts still cling to the mouldering past,
But the hopes of youth fall thick in the blast,
    And the days are dark and dreary.

Be still, sad heart! and cease repining;
Behind the clouds is the sun still shining;
Thy fate is the common fate of all,
Into each life some rain must fall
    Some days must be dark and dreary.

Henry Wadsworth Longfellow

COURAGE

If God be for us, who can be against us?   *Romans 8:31*

I can do all things through Christ that strengthened me.
                            Philippians 4:13

God hath not given us the spirit of fear; but of power, and
of love, and of a sound mind.   *II Timothy 1:7*

HE PRAYETH WELL

He prayeth well who loveth well
Both man and bird and beast;
He prayeth best who loveth best
All things both great and small;
For the dear God who loveth us,
He made and loveth all.

Samuel T. Coleridge

THE PHARISEE AND THE PUBLICAN

And he spake this parable unto certain which trusted in themselves that they were righteous, and despised others: Two men went up into the temple to pray; the one a Pharisee, and the other a publican. The Pharisee stood and prayed thus with himself, God, I thank thee, that I am not as other men are, extortioners, unjust, adulterers, or even as this publican. I fast twice in the week, I give tithes of all that I possess. And the publican, standing afar off, would not lift up so much as his eyes unto heaven, but smote upon his breast, saying, God be merciful to me a sinner. I tell you, this man went down to his house justified rather than the other: for every one that exalteth himself shall be abased; and he that humbleth himself shall be exalted. *Luke 18:9-14*

FORGIVENESS

For if ye forgive men their trespasses, your heavenly Father will also forgive you: but if he forgive not men their trespasses, neither will your Father forgive your trespasses.

Matthew 6:5-15

NATURE

As a fond mother, when the day is o'er
Leads by the hand her little child to bed,

Half willing, half reluctant to be led,
And leave his broken playthings on the floor.

Still gazing at them through the open door
  Nor wholly reassured and comforted
  By promises of others in their stead,
  Which though more splendid, may not please him more;

So Nature deals with us, and takes away our
  Playthings one by one, and by the hand
  Leads us to rest so gently, that we go

Scarce knowing if we wish to go or stay,
  Being too full of sleep to understand
  How far the unknown transcends what we know.

Henry Wadsworth Longfellow

BEWARE OF DESPERATE STEPS

Beware of desperate steps; the darkest day,
Lived till tomorrow, will have passed away.

William Cowper

CHILDREN AND PARENTS

Children, obey your parents in the Lord: for this is right.
Honor thy father and mother; which is the first commandment
with promise; That it may be well with thee, and thou mayest
live long on earth. And, ye fathers, provoke not your children
to wrath: but bring them up in the nurture and admonition of
the Lord. *Ephesians 6:1-4*

CHANGING SIGNS

This summer in New England I heard a story that I suppose
that most of us have heard at one time or another. It concerned
a man now grown old, who had graduated from one of our
Ivy League colleges. In his latter years he had given much
thought to his youth—the delights of those days, the hurts, the

wrongs, which had been perpetrated—and he was gravely concerned about a college prank that had been played then. After an unusually exciting football game, he and a group of other young men had driven through some of the nearby New England towns and had changed all the signs at the Commons and he was wondering, "how many people had gone down the wrong roads because he had changed the signs."

Change the signs of conscience and life is wrecked. Tell yourself that it is no longer necessary to be truthful, but that you can lie. Insist that honor is all right but immorality is permissible, that steadfastness is old-fashioned and expediency is profitable today, and life will be shipwrecked indeed. Every city is filled with men and women who are financially successful, who have achieved identification in their professions, but who in their success rose upon the dead stone of a conscience that could no longer speak. *Dr. Robert Lamont*

FAITH

An outward and visible sign of an inward and spiritual grace.

Book of Common Prayer

I have fought a good fight, I have finished my course, I have kept the faith. *II Timothy IV:7*

COURAGE

The Lord is my helper, and I will not fear what man shall do unto me. *Hebrews 13:6*

Perfect love casteth out fear. *I John 4:18*

Fight the good fight of faith, lay hold on eternal life, whereunto thou art also called, and hast professed a good profession before many witnesses. *I Timothy 6:12*

Watch ye, stand fast in the faith, quit you like men, be strong. *I Corinthians 16:13*

I STAY A LITTLE LONGER

Good-night! good-night! as we so oft have said,
  Beneath this roof at midnight, in the days
  That are no more, and shall no more return.
Thou hast but taken up thy lamp and gone to bed;
  I stay a little longer, as one stays
  To cover up the embers that still burn.

Henry Wadsworth Longfellow

GOD IS AWAKE

Have courage for the great sorrows of life and patience for the small ones; and when you have laboriously accomplished your daily task, go to sleep in peace. God is awake.

Victor Hugo

MY HANDICAPS

I thank God for my handicaps, for, through them, I have found myself, my work, and my God.   *Helen Keller*

NEVER GIVE UP

When you get into a tight place and everything goes against you, till it seems as though you could not hold on a minute longer, never give up then, for that is just the place and time that the tide will turn.   *Harriet Beecher Stowe*

LIFE

A useless life is only an early death.   *Goethe*

PRAYER

And I say unto you, Ask, and it shall be given you; seek, and ye shall find; knock, and it shall be opened unto you.

For every one that asketh receiveth; and he that seeketh findeth; and to him that knocketh it shall be opened. If a son shall ask bread of any of you that is a father, will he give him a stone? or if he ask a fish, will he for a fish give him a serpent? Of if he shall ask an egg, will he offer him a scorpion? If ye then, being evil, know how to give good gifts unto your children; how much more shall your heavenly Father give the Holy Spirit to them that ask him?   *Luke 11:9-13*

YE ARE THE TEMPLE OF GOD

Know ye not that ye are the temple of God, and that the Spirit of God dwelleth in you? If any man defile the temple of God, him shall God destroy; for the temple of God is holy, which temple ye are.   *I Corinthians 3:16-17*

BENEDICTIONS

The grace of the Lord Jesus Christ, and the love of God, and the communion of the Holy Ghost, be with you all. Amen.
          II Corinthians 13:14

And, lo, I am with you alway, even unto the end of the world. Amen.   *Matthew 28:20*

Finally, brethren, farewell. Be perfect, be of good comfort, be of one mind, live in peace; and the God of love and peace shall be with you.   *II Corinthians 13:11*

The Lord watch between me and thee, when we are absent one from another.   *Genesis 31:49*

Now the God of peace, that brought again from the dead our Lord Jesus, that great shepherd of the sheep, through the blood of the everlasting covenant, Make you perfect in every good work to do his will, working in you that which is well-

pleasing in his sight, through Jesus Christ; to whom be glory
for ever and ever. Amen.   *Hebrews 13:20-21*

HE KNOWS NOT

Who ne'er his bread in sorrow ate,
Who ne'er the mournful midnight hours
Weeping upon his bed has sate,
He knows you not, ye Heavenly Powers.   *Goethe*

TO GIVE AS I HAVE RECEIVED

How extraordinary is the situation of us mortals. Each of
us is here for a brief sojourn; for what purpose he knows not
though he sometimes thinks he senses it. But without going
deeper than our daily life, it is plain that we exist for our
fellow-men—in the first place for those upon whose smiles and
welfare our happiness depends, and next for all those unknown
to us personally but to whose destinies we are bound by the
tie of sympathy. A hundred times every day I remind myself
that my inner and outer life depend on the labors of other
men, living and dead, and that I must exert myself in order
to give in the measure as I have received and am still re-
ceiving.

SO LIVE

So live, that when thy summons comes to join
The innumerable caravan, which moves
To that mysterious realm, where each shall take
His chamber in the silent halls of death,
Thou go not, like the quarry-slave at night,
Scourged to his dungeon, but, sustained and soothed
By an unfaltering trust, approach thy grave
Like one who wraps the drapery of his couch
About him, and lies down to pleasant dreams.

William Cullen Bryant

THE POOR

Blessed is he that considereth the poor:
The Lord will deliver him in time of trouble.
The Lord will preserve him, and keep him alive;
And he shall be blessed upon the earth.

Psalm 41:1-2

COME UNTO ME

Come unto me, all ye that labor and are heavy laden; and
I will give you rest. Take my yoke upon you, and learn of
me; for I am meek and lowly in heart: and ye shall find rest
unto your souls. For my yoke is easy, and my burden is light.

Matthew 11:28-30

SORROW NOT

But I would not have you to be ignorant, brethren, con-
cerning them which are asleep, that ye sorrow not, even as
others which have no hope. For if we believe that Jesus died
and rose again, even so them also which sleep in Jesus will
God bring with him.   *I Thessalonians 4:13-14*

In my Father's house are many mansions . . . I go to pre-
pare a place for you.   *John 14:2*

THE WORLD PASSETH AWAY

If any man love the world, the love of the Father is not
in him. For all that is in the world, the lust of the flesh, and
the lust of the eyes, and the pride of life, is not of the Father,
but is of the world. And the world passeth away, and the
lust thereof: but he that doeth the will of God abideth for
ever.   *I John 2:15-17*

TAKE UP THE CROSS

Then said Jesus unto his disciples, If any man will come after me, let him deny himself, and take up his cross, and follow me. For whosoever will save his life shall lose it: and whosoever will lose his life for my sake shall find it. For what is a man profited, if he shall gain the whole world, and lose his own soul? or what shall a man give in exchange for his soul?   *Matthew 16:24-26*

THE CORNERSTONE

It is on the parched granite of pain that man has firmly established love and courage, heroism and pity. Suffering is the cornerstone of life. On it humanity is founded as on a firm rock. If it should disappear, it would take with it all that makes the worth of life, it would despoil the earth of its splendor and of its glory. It would tear from it the tremulous love of mothers and the piety of sons, it would banish knowledge along with study and would extinguish the lights of the mind.   *Anatole France*

DEATH

He is not dead, this friend; not dead,
But, in the path we mortals tread,
Got some few, trifling steps ahead,
　　And nearer to the end;
So that you, too, once past the bend
Shall meet again, as face to face this friend
You fancy dead.   *Robert Louis Stevenson*

THE WIDOW'S MITE

And Jesus sat over against the treasury, and beheld how the people cast money into the treasury: and many that were rich cast in much. And there came a certain poor widow, and she threw in two mites, which make a farthing. And he called

unto him his disciples, and saith unto them, Verily I say
unto you, That this poor widow hath cast more in, than all
they which have cast into the treasury: For all they did cast
in of their abundance; but she of her want did cast in all that
she had, even all her living.   *Mark 12:41-44*

OF SUCH IS THE KINGDOM

Then were there brought unto him little children, that he
should put his hands on them, and pray: and the disciples
rebuked them. But Jesus said, Suffer little children, and forbid
them not, to come unto me; for of such is the kingdom of
heaven. And he laid his hands on them, and departed hence.

Matthew 19:13-15

THE FIRST COMMUNION

For I have received of the Lord that which also I delivered
unto you, That the Lord Jesus, the same night in which he
was betrayed, took bread: And when he had given thanks, he
brake it, and said, Take, eat; this is my body, which is broken
for you: this do in remembrance of me. After the same manner also he took the cup, when he had supped, saying, This
cup is the new testament in my blood: this do ye, as oft as ye
drink it, in remembrance of me. For as often as ye eat this
bread, and drink this cup, ye do show the Lord's death till he
come.   *I Corinthians 11:23-26*

THE CHRIST-LIKE LIFE

And be ye kind one to another, tender-hearted, forgiving
one another, even as God for Christ's sake hath forgiven you.

Ephesians 4:32

LOVE

The night has a thousand eyes,
And the day but one;

Yet the light of the bright world dies
With the dying sun.

The mind has a thousand eyes,
  And the heart but one;
Yet the light of a whole life dies
  When love is done.   *F. W. Bourdillon*

LOVE'S YOUNG DREAM

There's nothing half so sweet in life
As love's young dream.   *Thomas Moore*

MAN

So God created man in his own image, in the image of God
created he him.   *Genesis I, 27*

I CAN'T

The only person who is always right is the one who says,
"I can't."

THE FAMILY AND WORSHIP SERVICES

The family should attend worship services in the sanctuary
regularly as a family. The children are more ready for public
worship than we think. They are older than we realize and
the time for teaching them is shorter than we imagine. The
family together in worship in the sanctuary is of greater value
than we will ever know. Dr. Albert Schweitzer in his *Memoirs
of Childhood and Youth* tells us that in his opinion the most
important thing his parents did for him when he was a child
was to take him to the worship services of the church.

> From the service in which I joined as a child, I have
> taken with me into life a feeling for what is solemn
> and a need for quiet and self-recollection without
> which I cannot realize the meaning of my life. I can-
> not therefore support the opinion of those who would

not let the children take part in grown-up people's services until they to some extent understood them. The important thing is not that they shall understand but that they shall feel something of what is serious and solemn. The fact that the child sees his parents full of devotion and has to feel something of devotion himself, that is what gives the service its meaning to him.

Don't worry about your child's behaviour in church. A four-year-old whose parents have a sincere feeling of reverence and worship in the sanctuary will be better behaved than some adults who squirm and twist, whisper and feel no sense of reverence in the presence of God. Worshipping together as a family in the sanctuary regularly is an essential in having a home.

The worship of God should be dignified and orderly. His house should reflect something of His majesty. The church school classes and activities should reflect careful thinking about God's revelation of Himself through Jesus Christ. God is concerned about all this, but He is undoubtedly more concerned about what happens in our houses than what happens in His. What we do at home, the attitudes we have, and the religion which determines our decisions are what we pass on to our children. What happens in the church building can be only added to or in conflict with what happens in our homes. It will never replace it!   *G. Raymond Campbell*

GOSSIP
There is no such thing as idle gossip. Gossip is always busy.

MEMORIES
Long, long be my heart with such memories fill'd!
Like the vase in which roses have once been distill'd:

You may break, you may shatter the vase if you will,
But the scent of the roses will hand around it still.

Thomas Moore

MERCY

Teach me to feel another's woe,
  To hide the fault I see;
That mercy I to others show,
  That mercy show to me.   *Pope*

IN A MYSTERIOUS WAY

God moves in a mysterious way
  His wonders to perform;
He plants his footsteps in the sea
  And rides upon the storm.

William Cowper

WHAT WE SHARE

Not what we give, but what we share,
For the gift without the giver is bare;
Who gives himself with his alms feeds three,
Himself, his hungering neighbor, and Me.

Lowell

THE GREATEST MOMENTS

You will find as you look back upon your life that the moments that stand out, the moments when you have really lived, are the moments when you have done things in a spirit of love.   *Henry Drummond*

GOD IS GOOD

I have no answer, for myself or thee,
Save that I learned beside my mother's knee:
"All is of God that is, and is to be;

And God is good." Let this suffice us still,
Resting in childlike trust upon his will
Who moves to his great ends unthwarted by the ill.

John Greenleaf Whittier

DREAMS

We grow great by dreams. All big men are dreamers. They see things in the soft haze of a spring day or in the red fire of a long winter's evening. Some of us let these great dreams die, but others nourish and protect them; nurse them through bad days till they bring them to the sunshine and light which comes always to those who hope that their dreams will come true. *Woodrow Wilson*

CONSIDER

Consider
The lilies of the field whose bloom is spring:—
We are as they;
Like them we fade away
As doth a leaf. *Christina Rossetti*

MOTHER

The angels . . . singing unto one another,
Can find among their burning terms of love,
None so devotional as that of "mother." *Poe*

YOUR FELLOW MAN

Even if it's a little thing, do something for those who have need of help, something for which you get no pay but the privilege of doing it. *Albert Schweitzer*

Till the war-drum throbb'd no longer and the battle-flags were
    furl'd
In the Parliament of man, the Federation of the World.

Tennyson

A TASK

To be honest, to be kind—to earn a little and to spend a
little less, to make upon the whole a family happier for his
presence, to renounce when that shall be necessary and not be
embittered, to keep a few friends, but these without capitula-
tion—above all, on the same grim condition, to keep friends
with himself—here is a task for all that a man has of fortitude
and delicacy.   *Robert Louis Stevenson*

THE WINTER IS PAST

Lo, the winter is past, the rain is over and gone:
    the flowers appear on the earth;
The time of the singing of the birds is come:
    and the voice of the turtle is heard in the land.
The fig-tree ripeneth her green figs:
    and the vines are in blossom,
    they give forth their fragrance.

Song of Solomon II

BE NOT ANXIOUS

Therefore I say unto you, Be not anxious for your life. What
ye shall eat, or what ye shall drink; not yet for your body,
what ye shall put on. Is not the life more than the food, and
the body than raiment? Your heavenly Father knoweth that
ye have need of all these things.   *Matthew VI*

THREE CLASSES

All mankind is divided into three classes: those that are
immovable, those that are movable, and those that move.

Arabian Proverb

THREE STEPS

There are three steps leading to the place where harmony lives, yet they are hard to climb. The first is to think kindly of one's neighbor. The second is to speak kindly to him. The third is to act kindly toward him. The reason they are hard to climb is that we are too busily engaged in thinking well of ourselves, speaking well of ourselves, and acting in a manner which we think will do ourselves the most good.

HIS TRAINING

I was trained from the beginning to work, to save, and to give. *John D. Rockefeller, Jr.*

A PRAYER

Lord, make me an instrument of Thy Peace. Where there is hatred, let me sow love; where there is injury, pardon; where there is doubt, faith; where there is despair, hope; where there is darkness, light; and where there is sickness, joy. O Divine Master, grant that I may not so much seek to be consoled as to console; to be understood as to understand; to be loved as to love; for it is in giving that we receive; it is in pardoning that we are pardoned; and it is in dying that we are born to eternal life.

Prayer of St. Francis of Assissi

FORGETTING SELF

To me there is in happiness an element of self-forgetfulness. You lose yourself in something outside yourself when you are happy; just as when you are desperately miserable you are intensely conscious to yourself, are a solid little lump of ego weighing a ton. *J. B. Priestley*

OUR HEARTS UNTO WISDOM

Lord, thou hast been our dwelling-place in all generations. Before the mountains were brought forth, or ever thou hadst formed the earth and the world, even from everlasting to everlasting, thou art God.

Thou turnest man to destruction, and sayest, Return, ye children of men. For a thousand years in thy sight are but as yesterday when it is passed, and as a watch in the night.

Thou carriest them away as with a flood; they are as a sleep: in the morning they are like grass which groweth up. In the morning it flourisheth, and groweth up; in the evening it is cut down, and withereth.

The days of our years are threescore years and ten, or even by reason of strength, fourscore years; yet is their pride but labor and sorrow, for it is soon gone, and we fly away.

So teach us to number our days, that we may apply our hearts unto wisdom.   *Psalm 90:1-6, 10, 12*

THE ROOT OF ALL HAPPINESS

I believe the root of all happiness on this earth to lie in the realization of a spiritual life with a consciousness of something wider than materialism; in the capacity to live in a world that makes you unselfish because you are not over anxious about your personal place; that makes you tolerant because you realize your own comic fallibilities; that gives you tranquillity without complacency because you believe in something so much larger than yourself.   *Sir Hugh Walpole*

CONTENTMENT

The secret of contentment is the discovery by every man of his own powers and limitations, finding satisfaction in a line of activity which he can do well, plus the wisdom to know that his place, no matter how important or successful he is, never counts very much in the universe. A man may very well be so successful in carving a name for himself in his field that he begins to imagine himself indispensable or omnipotent. He is eaten up by some secret ambition, and then good-bye to all contentment. Sometimes it is more important to discover what one cannot do than what one can do. So much restlessness is due to the fact that a man does not know what he wants, or he wants too many things, or perhaps he wants to be somebody else, to be anybody except himself. The courage of being one's genuine self, of standing alone and of not wanting to be somebody else!   *Lin Yutang*

OBJECTIVES IN LIFE

The greedy search for money or success will almost always lead men into unhappiness. Why? Because that kind of life makes them depend upon things outside themselves.

Andre Maurois

THE GOLDEN PRESENT

One important source of unhappiness is the habit of putting off living to some fictional future date. Men and women are constantly making themselves unhappy because in deferring their lives to the future they lose sight of the present and its golden opportunities for rich living.   *W. Beran Wolfe*

UNDER THE STARS

It takes solitude, under the stars, for us to be reminded of our eternal origin and our far destiny.   *Archibald Rutledge*

ABIDE WITH ME

Abide with me; fast falls the eventide;
The darkness deepens; Lord, with me abide;
When other helpers fail, and comforts flee,
Help of the helpless, oh abide with me.

Swift to its close ebbs out life's little day;
Earth's joys grow dim, its glories pass away;
Change and decay in all around I see;
O Thou who changest not, abide with me.

I need Thy presence every passing hour;
What but Thy grace can foil the tempter's power?
Who like Thyself my guide and stay can be?
Through cloud and sunshine, Lord, abide with me.

I fear no foe with Thee at hand to bless;
Ills have no weight, and tears no bitterness;
Where is death's sting? where, grave, thy victory?
I triumph still, if Thou abide with me.

Hold then Thy cross before my closing eyes;
Shine through the gloom, and point me to the skies;
Heaven's morning breaks, and earth's vain shadows flee;
In life, in death, O Lord, abide with me.

Henry Francis Lyte

COME UNTO ME

Come unto me, all ye who labor and are heavy laden, and
I will give you rest. *Matthew 11:28*

FAITH

I will lift up mine eyes unto the hills, from whence cometh
my help.
My help cometh from the Lord, which made Heaven and
earth.
He will not suffer thy foot to be moved: He that keepeth thee
will not slumber.
Behold, He that keepeth Israel·shall neither slumber nor sleep.
The Lord is thy keeper: the Lord is thy shade upon thy right
hand.
The sun shall not smite thee by day, nor the moon by night.
The Lord shall preserve thee from all evil: He shall preserve
thy soul.
The Lord shall preserve thy going out and thy coming in from
this time forth, and even for evermore. *Psalms 121*

IN THE MORNING

What is our death but a night's sleep? For as through sleep
all weariness and faintness pass away and cease, and the powers
of the spirit come back again, so that in the morning we arise
fresh and strong and joyous; so at the Last Day we shall rise
again as if we had only slept a night, and shall be fresh and
strong.   *Martin Luther*

HANDS OF PRAYER

More things are wrought by prayer
Than this world dreams of. Whereof, let thy voice
Rise like a fountain for me night and day.
For what are men better than sheep or goats
That nourish a blind life within the brain.
If, knowing God, they lift not hands of prayer
Both for themselves and those who call them friend?

Alfred Tennyson

COURAGE

To struggle when hope is banished!
To live when life's salt is gone!
To dwell in a dream that's vanished—
To endure, and go calmly on!   *Ben Jonson*

GRIEF

It is dangerous to abandon one's self to the luxury of grief;
it deprives one of courage, and even of the wish for recovery.

Henri F. Amiel

OVERCOMING DISABILITY

I discovered early that the hardest thing to overcome is not
a physical disability but the mental condition which it in-
duces. The world, I found, has a way of taking a man pretty

much at his own rating. If he permits his loss to make him embarrassed and apologetic, he will draw embarrassment from others. But if he gains his own respect, the respect of those around him comes easily.   *Major Alexander P. de Seversky*

DEATH

Death, be not proud, though some have called thee
Mighty and dreadful, for thou art not so:
For those whom thou think'st thou dost overthrow
Die not, poor Death, nor yet canst thou kill me.
From rest and sleep, which but thy pictures be,
Much pleasure, then from thee much more must flow;
And soonest our best men with thee do go—
Rest of their bones and souls' delivery!
Thou'rt slave to fate, chance, kings, and desperate men,
And dost with poison, war, and sickness dwell;
And poppy or charms can make us sleep as well,
And better than thy stroke. Why swell'st thou then?
    One short sleep past, we wake eternally,
    And Death shall be no more: Death, thou shalt die.

John Donne

WORK ON

Never despair. But if you do, work on in despair.

Edmund Burke

OUR TRUST FIXED ON GOD

We shall steer safely through every storm, so long as our heart is right, our intention fervent, our courage steadfast, and our trust fixed on God. If at times we are somewhat stunned by the tempest, never fear, let us take breath, and go on afresh.   *Francis de Sales*

HE IS NOT ELEVATED

Did you ever hear of a man who had striven all his life faithfully and singly toward an object and in no measure obtained it? If a man constantly aspires, is he not elevated?

Henry David Thoreau

PERSEVERANCE

Perseverance is a great element of success. If you only knock long enough and loud enough at the gate, you are sure to wake up somebody.

Henry Wadsworth Longfellow

THE GREATEST MISTAKE

It is the greatest of all mistakes to do nothing because you can only do a little. Do what you can.   *Sydney Smith*

THINGS WORK OUT

So long as one does not despair, so long as one doesn't look upon life bitterly, things work out fairly well in the end.

George Moore

LET US DO GOOD

As we have therefore opportunity, let us do good unto all men.   *Galatians 6:10*

HELPING ANOTHER

It is one of the most beautiful compensations of this life that no man can sincerely try to help another without helping himself.   *Ralph Waldo Emerson*

LIFE IS SHORT

Life is short and we have not too much time for gladdening
the hearts of those who are traveling the dark way with us.
Oh, be swift to love! Make haste to be kind!

Henri F. Amiel

FORGIVENESS

In this life, if you have anything to pardon, pardon quickly.
Slow forgiveness is little better than no forgiveness.

Sir Arthur W. Pinero

I FORGAVE

My heart was heavy, for its trust had been
Abused, its kindness answered with foul wrong;
So turning gloomily from my fellow men,
One summer Sabbath day I strolled among
The green mounds of the village burial-place;
Where, pondering how all human love and hate
Find one sad level; and how, soon or late,
Wronged and wrongdoer, each with meekened face,
And cold hands folded over a still heart,
Pass the green threshold of our common grave,
Whither all footsteps tend, whence none depart,
Awed for myself, and pitying my race,
Our common sorrow, like a mighty wave,
Swept all my pride away, and, trembling, I forgave!

John Greenleaf Whittier

EACH MAN'S LIFE

If we could read the secret history of our enemies we should
find in each man's life sorrow and suffering enough to disarm
all hostility. *Henry Wadsworth Longfellow*

HUMAN AFFAIRS

Nothing in human affairs is worth any great anxiety.

Plato

THE BURDEN OF TOMORROW

It has been well said that no man ever sank under the burden of the day. It is when tomorrow's burden is added to the burden of today that the weight is more than a man can bear. Never load yourselves so, my friends. If you find yourselves so loaded, at least remember this: it is your own doing, not God's. He begs you to leave the future to Him, and mind the present. *George MacDonald*

TOMORROW

Finish each day and be done with it . . . You have done what you could: some blunders and absurdities no doubt crept in; forget them as soon as you can. Tomorrow is a new day; you shall begin it well and serenely.

Ralph Waldo Emerson

THE FAMILY

Lord, behold our family here assembled. We thank Thee for this place in which we dwell; for the love that unites us; for the peace accorded us this day; for the hope with which we expect the morrow; for the health, the work, the food, and the bright skies that make our lives delightful; for our friends in all parts of the earth, and our friendly helpers in this foreign isle . . .

Give us courage, gaiety, and the quiet mind. Spare to us our friends, soften to us our enemies. Bless us, if it may be, in all our innocent endeavors. If it may not, give us the strength to encounter that which is to come, that we be brave in peril, constant in tribulation, temperate in wrath, and in all changes of fortune and down to the gates of death, loyal and loving one to another. Amen.

Robert Louis Stevenson

HOPE

And step by step, since time began,
I see the steady gain of man.

John Greenleaf Whittier

THIS IS MY COUNTRY

God grant that not only the love of liberty but a thorough knowledge of the rights of man may pervade all the nations of the earth, so that a philosopher may set his foot anywhere on its surface and say: "This is my country!"

Benjamin Franklin

PEACE

They shall beat their swords into plowshares, and their spears into pruning-hooks; nation shall not lift up sword against nation, neither shall they learn war any more.

Isaiah 2:4

THE RESPONSIBILITY OF PARENTS

For a long time parents fooled themselves into thinking they could preserve their children's individuality and responsibility for choice by not identifying their children with any religion. When their children grew up, parents claimed, they would be able to make their own choice of religious faith. That usually meant that the children went unbaptized, attended Sunday School spasmodically, and drifted from church to church, if they went at all, with no basic beliefs about God. Parents thought they were right in not giving their children a religion. What parents did not realize was that they were actually giving their children a religion, and a poor religion at that. Inevitably parents give their children the attitudes, values, and beliefs by which they live, and that is what religion is.

It may be a poor religion, centered on material possessions, and measured by dollar signs, regularly worshipped at the bank and expressed in the faith that money and gadgets will bring peace and happiness. It may be a conceited religion, centered on the individual himself, committed to personal desires, and characterized by scornful indifference to others. It may be an ethical religion, centered on law, both Biblical and civil, and expressing itself in personal honesty, individual integrity, and a sense of reponsibility. Or it may be the Christian religion, centered on the love of God, shown in the life, teaching, death, and resurrection of Jesus Christ, expressed in putting the needs of others before one's own, dying to oneself and coming alive to others, and in loving God by loving other people in the everyday contacts of life.

The basic, determining factors in the day-by-day living of parents make up their religion, and it is this that they pass on to their children. Boys and girls can be reared with no more vacuum in their spirits than in their stomachs. So the old idea of "no religion" was ignorance. Inevitably, unconsciously, and without question parents pass on to their children their own God or gods.

The Reverend G. Raymond Campbell

PRAYER

He prayeth best who loveth best
All things both great and small;
For the dear God, who loveth us,
He made and loveth all.   *S. T. Coleridge*

BE GOOD TO ME

When the last sea is sailed and the last shallow charted,
When the last field is reaped and the last harvest stored,

When the last fire is out and the last guest departed,
  Grant the last prayer that I shall pray, Be good to me, O
    Lord. *Masefield*

THE LAST KIND WORD

'Twas a thief said the last kind word to Christ;
Christ took the kindness and forgave the theft.

R. Browning

THINK ON THESE THINGS

Whatsoever things are true, whatsoever things are honest,
whatsoever things are just, whatsoever things are pure, whatsoever things are lovely, whatsoever things are of good report:
if there be any virtue, and if there be any praise, think on
these things. *Philippians IV, 8*

ON WINGS OF DEEDS

On wings of deeds the soul must mount!
  When we are summoned from afar,
Ourselves, and not our words will count—
  Not what we said, but what we are!

William Winter

FOR OTHERS

What we have done for ourselves alone, dies with us; what
we have done for others and the world, remains and is immortal. *Albert Pike*

ENEMIES

Enemies are never truly conquered until their friendship
is won. *Wilferd Peterson*

THE CHALLENGE

The sum of the whole matter is this: our civilization cannot survive materially unless it be redeemed spiritually. It can be saved only by the practices that spring out of that spirit. Here is the final challenge to our churches, and to every one who fears God or loves his country.   *Woodrow Wilson*

THE GOSPEL OF PEACE

Give me the money that has been spent in war and I will clothe every man, woman, and child in an attire of which kings and queens will be proud. I will build a schoolhouse in every valley over the whole earth. I will crown every hillside with a place of worship consecrated to the gospel of peace.

Charles Sumner

"DOES GOD LIVE HERE?"

A stranger came walking along the dusty road, opened the gate, walked up the path to the door of the farmhouse and knocked. The farmer's wife answered the door. She expected to see a neighborhood friend, but it was a stranger standing there. He asked, "Does God live here?"

The woman was perplexed and dumbfounded, and did not answer. Again the stranger asked, "Does God live here?" But the woman was so confused that she could not answer. And the third time the man asked, "Does God live here?" But there was no answer, and instead, the woman slammed the door and ran out of the back of the house. The man shook his head, turned, and walked away.

At the barn, where the husband was working, the wife told him excitedly of the strange visitor. The husband blustered and floundered for words. He finally said, "Well, didn't you tell him we belong to the church?"

"No," answered the wife conscientiously, "that wasn't what he asked."

"Well, didn't you tell him I'm a deacon, and you're a member of the Women's Missionary Society?"

But she answered, "No, that wasn't what he asked."

Together they pondered over the strange visitor, and the meaning of his mysterious question. And they came to the conclusion that perhaps their home was not a place where God could live.

Centuries before there was a state, or a school, or a church, homes were instituted as places where men and women should live together in love and happiness; where children should be reared into worthy lives. But many enemies threaten the home today—disrespect, disloyalty, lack of Christian atmosphere, little religious training, little or no Christian literature. Many parents have become lax in their discipline; in their fear of being old-fashioned, they are permitting their children to do things that are not only questionable, but often demoralizing and dangerous.

Our homes need to get back to God's standard. We need to exalt the sacredness of the marriage tie; we need to make our homes a place of sobriety, and righteousness, and unfailing love. This sacred institution should be so filled with honor and righteousness, that no stranger need ask, "Does God live here?"   *Sunshine Magazine*

WHAT IS YOURS

Remember that what you possess in the world will be found at the day of your death to belong to another, but what you are will be yours forever.   *Henry van Dyke*

LIVING AND GIVING

We make a living by what we get, but we make a life by what we give.

CHECK UP OCCASIONALLY

It's good to have money, and the things that money can buy, but it's good, too, to check up once in a while and be sure you haven't lost the things money can't buy.

George Horace Lorimer

IF THERE IS—

The Chinese have a proverb, in fact a precept, which if carried to fruition would cure the ills of the world. It is this:

"If there is righteousness in the heart, there will be beauty in the character. If there is beauty in the character, there will be harmony in the home. If there is harmony in the home, there will be order in the nation. If there is order in the nation, there will be peace in the world."

THE TWO VOICES

An old Indian once bought some things from a white man who kept a store. When he got back to his wigwam and opened the bundles, he found some money inside one of them.

"Good luck!" thought the old Indian to himself. "I will keep this money. It will buy many more things."

He went to bed, but he could not sleep. All night he was thinking of the money. Over and over again he thought, "I will keep it. I will keep it for my own." But something within him seemed to say, "No you must not keep it, that would not be right."

Early the next morning he went back to the white man's store. "Here is money," he said; "I found it."

"Why didn't you keep it?" asked the storekeeper.

"There are two voices inside of me," replied the Indian. "One said, 'Keep it, you found it, and the white man will never know.'

"Then the other said, 'Take it back! Take it back! It is not yours. You have no right to keep it.'

"Then the first one said, 'Keep it! Keep it! You are foolish to take it back.'

"But the other voice spoke more loudly, 'No, no! Take it back!'

"The two voices inside me talked all night and would not let me sleep. Now the two voices will stop talking. Tonight I shall sleep."

THE RIGHT PATH

Because a path is difficult and dangerous, we must not avoid it, but only ask if it be the right path.

MY HOPE

By profession I am a soldier, and take pride in that fact. But I am more proud, infinitely more, to be a father. A soldier destroys in order to build; a father only builds, never destroys. The one has the potentialities of death, the other embodies creation and life. While the hordes of death are mighty, the battalions of life are mightier still. It is my hope that my son, when I am gone, will remember me not from the battles, but in the home, repeating with him our simple daily prayer, "Our Father, who art in heaven."

Gen. Douglas MacArthur

INSPIRATION

The great composer does not set to work because he is inspired, but becomes inspired because he is working. Beethoven, Wagner, Bach, and Mozart settled down day after day to the job in hand with as much regularity as an accountant settles down each day in his figures. They didn't waste time waiting for inspiration.   *Ernest Newman*

THE ETERNAL GOODNESS

I know not where His islands lift
  Their fronded palms in air;

I only know I cannot drift
  Beyond His love and care.
O brothers! If my faith is vain,
  If hopes like these betray.
Pray for me that my feet may gain
  The sure and safer way.
And Thou, O Lord! by whom are seen
  Thy creatures as they be,
Forgive me if too close I lean
  My human heart on Thee.

John Greenleaf Whittier

BE NOBLE

Be noble! and the nobleness that lies
In other men, sleeping, but never dead,
Will rise in majesty to meet thine own.

Lowell

CHRIST GLORIFIED THE COMMON TASK

Christ washed the disciples' feet (John 13:1-12). Consider these facts of the foot-washing in the Upper Room and apply them to your problems of work. We all try to follow Jesus in Communion; we do that eagerly, but remember, Jesus washed their feet before He ever instituted His Communion Supper. And that may be a most significant procedure. Most of us need the humility and desire to serve before we come to His table. Here are some deep, searching facts: 1. He did what others had neglected or refused to do. 2. He did what others felt they were too good to do. 3. He rebuked their foolish and childish pride. 4. He did it, because it was necessary—someone had to do it. 5. He washed the feet of Judas, the man who was going to betray him. Many have the task day after day of washing the feet of some Judas. 6. He did the hated job in such a gracious way, He captured their admiration and respect. 7. He acted! He didn't argue, criticize or condemn; He just did that which had to be done.   *Dr. Clinton C. Cox*

BRIGHTER SHINE

At sixty-two life has begun;
  At seventy-three begin once more;
Fly swifter as thou near'st at the sun,
  And brighter shine at eighty-four,
    At ninety-five
    Shouldst thou arrive,
Still wait on God, and work and thrive.

Oliver Wendell Holmes

GOD

God is to me that creative force, behind and in the universe, who manifests himself as energy, as life, as order, as beauty, as thought, as conscience, as love, and who is self-revealed supremely in the creative Person of Jesus of Nazareth, and operative in all Jesus-like movements in the world today.

Henry Sloane Coffin

THY TRUTH

Grant us thy truth to make us free,
And kindling hearts that burn for thee;
Till all thy living altars claim
One holy light, one heavenly flame.

Oliver Wendell Holmes

ALONE

Naked and alone we came into exile . . . which of us has known his brother? Which of us has looked into his father's heart? . . . which of us is not forever a stranger and alone?

Thomas Wolfe

"GOD BLESS US EVERY ONE"

All the blessed sentiments of Christmas dwell in these words of Tiny Tim. Good will is there, gratitude to God, the soulful sense of the brotherhood of man, that divine spark of unselfishness which glows supreme in the Yuletide, though it may be smothered with ashes in all the rest of the year.

"Every one" allows no exceptions. The rich, the poor, the kind, the cruel, the good, the bad—all are included. All do not deserve the divine blessing equally, but all need it equally, and in their several ways may be touched and purified and lifted up, for the moment at least to a realization of the spiritual meaning of life.   *Sunshine Magazine*

TO BE ABLE

To be able to bear an injustice without retaliating. To be able to do one's duty even when one is not watched. To be able to keep at the job until it is finished. To be able to make use of criticism without letting it defeat you.

AFFLICTION

It has done me good to be somewhat parched by the heat and drenched by the rain of life.   *Longfellow*

God sometimes washes the eyes of his children with tears that they may read aright his providence and his commandments.   *T. L. Cuyler*

It is not from the tall, crowded workhouse of prosperity that men first or clearest see the eternal stars of heaven.

Theodore Parker

THE LORD IS MY SHEPHERD

Dr. Samuel Lindsey, of Brookline, Mass., tells that his mother always began every day by reciting to herself the first verse of the 23rd Psalm: "The Lord is my Shepherd, I shall not want." This she did till the morning of her 80th birthday. On that morning, and every morning after that until she went home to realize its fulfillment, she began the day by reciting the last verse of the Psalm: "Surely goodness and mercy shall follow me all the days of my life, and I will dwell in the house of the Lord forever." Think of the peace and poise she must have contributed to her life by that simple, little habit. And that, in part, is the value of a "quiet time" in which one reads his Bible and then sits for a moment of quiet meditation and prayer, giving God a chance to walk through his mind, refreshing the parched places, and causing them to spring up into flower gardens of inspiration and faith.

Clarence W. Cranford

AGE

I venerate old age; and I love not the man who can look without emotion upon the sunset of life, when the dusk of evening begins to gather over the watery eye, and the shadows of twilight grow broader and deeper upon the understanding.

Longfellow

It is only necessary to grow old to become more charitable and even indulgent.—I see no fault committed by others that I have not committed myself. *Goethe*

ANGER

He best keeps from anger who remembers that God is always looking upon him. *Plato*

I OFFER HARDSHIP AND VICTORY

Setting out to liberate Italy, Garibaldi saw some young men at a street corner, and summoned them to enlist in the cause.

"What do you offer?" they asked.

"Offer?" replied Garibaldi. "I offer you hardship, hunger,

rags, thirst, sleepless nights, footsores in the long marches, privations innumerable, and victory in the noblest cause that ever asked you." Young Italy followed him.

And Jesus says: "If any one would come after Me, let him take up his cross, and follow Me."   *John S. Wimbish*

THE BIBLE

The Bible is one of the greatest blessings bestowed by God on the children of men. It has God for its author; salvation for its end, and truth without any mixture for its matter. It is all pure, all sincere; nothing too much; nothing wanting.   *Locke*

WHEN YOU HAVE READ IT

When you have read the Bible, you will know it is the word of God, because you will have found it the key to your own heart, your own happiness and your own duty.

Woodrow Wilson

THE PURPOSE OF A SERMON

What is a sermon for but to do two things. First, it should comfort the afflicted and second, it should afflict the comfortable. Sometimes the sermon does one thing and sometimes another.   *John Homer Miller*

THE HEARTHSTONE OF GOD

The city dweller is sentenced to push his way through unbrotherly crowds, jostling his fellows as he trudges along at the base of dark canyons between the towering skyscrapers. He seldom sees the skies. Sunrise and sunset are denied him. At church he may hear the minister read from the Psalms, "The heavens declare the glory of God"; but he is forced to take the preacher's word for it. The wandering nomads of our urban communities pitch their tents in neighborless apartments and rush headlong into the subways to burrow their way to work. The poets of the city may sing of steel and smoke, but the Psalmist declares "The heavens are the work of thy hands."

For the soul's good, it is wise to leave the cities occasionally, and those who are privileged to live in the country and look toward peaceful horizons should rejoice.

During recent days, I have journeyed through New England. Color is coming to the trees, and tomorrow the hillsides will be ablaze. A master hand is at work. He is prodigal with his paints, and has splashed the scarlets and carmine upon every lone maple. This year he seems to have unusual fondness for metals, and they are full of lustre, gold and brass and copper and bronze. One evening, as I drove along, I was startled. Suddenly the colors seemed to fade. The lustre left the metals, and the countryside took on a sombre hue. I was puzzled for a moment, and then understood. A sunset had burst upon us, and the flaming reds outshone the autumn trees and left them discontented in the shadows. I had never seen a sunset like it. I have seen the sky piled high with the crimson clouds of Wyoming. I have seen sunsets like the illuminated fountains of Versailles blazing with an inner light. But this sunset differed from them all. It burned like the low fires of a family hearth, blood red like coals upon which the bellows blow; here and there a ruby flash like coals breaking asunder or glowing logs falling apart. The clouds were like smoke from an altar ascending toward the heavens. On either side the skies were azure blue. The hearthstone of God!

The fire on this hearth burned unhurriedly. There was a timeless quality about it all. The colors lingered, just as the reflection of the red maples had been content to pause upon the surface of quiet pools in the early afternoon. For half an hour, it seemed we sat about this hearth before the hearthstone of God.

The world is full of prodigal sons who, far from the father's home, have yet to come to themselves and resolve, "I will return to my father's house." The hearthstone of God is ample, and the return of brothers everywhere in the reunion of mankind is imperative. The separated sons of the Father, as sons belonging to one family, but beneath the banners of class or of race or of nation. These concepts are too small to unite men in enduring peace.

It is rightful for a man to have a deep and abiding love for his country. My heart beats faster when I think of "purple mountain majesties," of "spacious skies," and "fruited plain." I am proud of "heroes proved in liberating strife," and glory in "the patriot's dream that sees beyond the years our alabaster cities undimmed by human tears." But I know that if our good is to be "crowned with brotherhood," patriotism, which is one of the holiest of emotions, must be ruled by the moral law. Men blindly seek union upon the basis of color or of race. Discussion ceases to be rational. Fires of hatred consume the caution of reason. No wonder realistic writers are full of pessimism, and predict the passing of our civilization. Is it naive or is it the sternest of realism to summon mankind to a reunion of the family at the hearthstone of God?

At the hearthstone of God, we look into the face of the Eternal. In the family reunions of yesterday, the father led in prayer. There were those wonderful moments of worship in which we knelt, realizing we were indeed members of one family but likewise children of God. It was a little harder to hold a grudge against a brother when we had knelt in prayer and had heard our father's voice. Jesus went beyond this, and commanded us to leave our gifts at the altar and be right with our brothers before attempting to worship. There is need throughout the earth for brethren who have dealt deceitfully with each other to become right with their brethren. Perhaps it is necessary to kneel first before the hearthstone of God. There must be repentance. There can be no reunion of the family of God, unless the sins of all members of the family are confessed, forgiveness found, and resolves there made to become right with one's brother. At the moment, statesmen bitterly denounce statesmen; sources of public information are fouled; propaganda reaches the people; the wells of hatred overflow; and men reach for their weapons.

G. Bromley Oxnam

INSPIRED

I know the Bible is inspired because it finds me at greater depths of my being than any other book.   *Coleridge*

EVERY CHILD

Every child born into the world is a new thought of God, an ever-fresh and radiant possibility.   *Kate Douglas Wiggin*

LET CHILDREN REMEMBER

Let all children remember, if ever they are weary of laboring for their parents, that Christ labored for his; if impatient of their commands, that Christ cheerfully obeyed; if reluctant to provide for their parents, that Christ forgot himself and provided for his mother amid the agonies of the crucifixion. The affectionate language of this divine example to every child is, "Go thou and do likewise."   *Dwight*

THE CHRISTIAN FAITH

The Christian faith reposes in a person rather than a creed. Christ is the personal, living center of theology, around which the whole Christian system is ensphered. Christ is the personal source of the individual Christian life; the personal head of the whole Christian church; the personal sovereign of the kingdom of grace.   *R. B. Welch*

GOD AND THY NEIGHBOR

Flatter not thyself in thy faith in God, if thou hast not charity for thy neighbor; I think not thou hast charity for thy neighbor, if thou wantest faith in God. Where they are not both together, they are both wanting; they are both dead if once divided.   *Quarles*

THE BEST PORTION OF A MAN'S LIFE

In those lines written above Tintern Abbey we are reminded of

> "That best portion of a good man's life,—
> His little, nameless, unremembered acts
> Of kindness and of love."

I sometimes wonder just what Wordsworth meant by "un-remembered." Does he mean that these acts of kindness and of love are unremembered by the recipient of them, or by the doer of them? I suppose it is the latter. That is undoubtedly what Jesus had in mind in the great judgment scene. There were those who appeared before the king in judgment who apparently had forgotten some of the acts and deeds of mercy which they had done in life, for when he said to them, "Come, ye blessed of my father, inherit the kingdom prepared for you from the foundation of the world: for I was an hungred and ye gave me meat; I was thirsty and ye gave me drink: I was a stranger and ye took me in, naked and ye clothed me: I was sick and ye visited me: I was in prison and ye came unto me," they answered, "Lord, when saw we thee an hungred and fed thee, and thirsty and gave thee drink; when saw we thee a stranger and took thee in, or naked and clothed thee; or when saw we thee sick and in prison and came unto thee?" But the king answered and said unto them, "Inasmuch as ye have done it unto one of the least of these my brethren, ye have done it unto me." How bitter and distressing it would be in the judgment to be confronted by unkind deeds that we had done, and forgotten; but how pleasing it will be to be reminded of acts of kindness and of love which we have done, and then forgotten!

Clarence Edward Macartney

HUMILITY

If thou wouldst find much favor and peace with God and man, be very low in thine own eyes. Forgive thyself little and others much.   *Leighton*

KINDNESS

When death, the great reconciler, has come, it is never our tenderness that we repent of, but our severity.   *George Eliot*

A CUP OF COLD WATER

One of the tremendous and moving scenes in Victor Hugo's "Notre Dame," is the scourging and torturing of Quasi Modo on the wheel. A great throng gathered about the pillory to witness, and alas, rejoice in the terrible spectacle. The hunchback, Quasi Modo, almost as much an animal in appearance as a man, was chained and strapped to the wheel, which turned horizontally on the platform, so that those standing on every side could behold the agony of the unfortunate man. As the wheel began to revolve the professional torturer took his whip and began to scourge Quasi Modo, whose desperate efforts to get free were all in vain. With the blood flowing from his wounds and wetting the platform, the hunchback moaned aloud for water. But the mob mocked him and threw missiles at him, stones and broken pitchers and decayed vegetables. In the midst of this terrible scene a young girl pushed her way through the crowd with a gourd in her hand, and, with a flaming look at the crowd, put the gourd of water to the lips of the sufferer. Then, what imprecations and missiles and whips could not do, this act of that young girl did. A look of astonishment came over the face of the hunchback, and after that a tear, perhaps the first he had ever shed, came slowly down his cheek. So Jesus said, "And whosoever shall give to drink unto one of these little ones a cup of cold water only in the name of a disciple, verily I say unto you he shall in no wise lose his reward."

Clarence Edward Macartney

COUNT THAT LOST

I count all that part of my life lost which I spent not in communion with God, or in doing good.   *Donne*

RESPONSIBILITY

A pastor friend of mine who was recently preparing for the marriage of his second daughter, the older daughter having already married, said to me, "I am beginning to realize how little time I gave to my children;" and he added, "If I had to do it all over again, I think perhaps I would spend a little more time with them even if a few details of my official responsibilities had to be neglected." We are reminded of that verse in the Song of Solomon where the author says, "They made me the keeper of the vineyards; but mine own vineyard have I not kept."   *Edward Hughes Pruden*

MARRIAGE

What greater thing is there for two human souls than to feel that they are joined for life—to strengthen each other in all labor, to rest on each other in all sorrow, to minister to each other in all pain, to be one with each other in silent, unspeakable memories at the moment of the last parting. *George Eliot*

ANDREW, SIMON PETER'S BROTHER

As the artist with the stroke of the brush brings the canvas to life, so Scripture has revealed to us the picture of this noble man. We are all familiar with the facts, but as we seek to honor his memory, let us briefly recall one or two of them.

Andrew strikes a responsive cord in us because he was an ordinary man like you or me. He was not a great preacher like

Peter. He was not a financial man like Matthew. He was not a great statesman like James who presided over the Council at Jerusalem. He was not a devout mystic and writer like John. He was just a plain ordinary fellow, so ordinary that everyone knew him as Simon Peter's brother. No doubt it was not easy for Andrew to play second fiddle to his brother. It is human nature for us to want to be on top of the pile.

John Jowett was right when he said that we all want to be stars when our Lord wants us to be street lamps. We want to stand in royal palaces and be cup bearers to the King, while all the time the King is saying, "Give a cup of cold water in my name."

Our weak human nature demands that we be somebody. Even so great a man as Henry Ward Beecher could not tolerate the notoriety Harriet Beecher Stowe received when *Uncle Tom's Cabin* appeared. In the Beecher family there was room for only one prominent person and that was Henry Ward.

Andrew accepted his allotted station but made the most of it. He had caught a humble attitude of life from Him who had once said, "He that would be greatest among you, let him be the servant of all." Andrew had the spirit of his Master.

If our Lord was preaching to us today, I can hear him say, "Quo Vadis? Whither goest thou? What are you after? What are you seeking? Too many of you are intoxicated with the lust to be somebody in the eyes of the world. You are running pell mell after money, position and power. I do not wonder that so many of you have stomach ulcers. The psychiatrists are reaping a harvest from you because your minds are out of order. You need to be still and know that the Lord He is God. You need to have the eyes of your soul enlightened. Take a little time to learn of me. 'My yoke is easy and my burden is light.' The things which you think are so important are incidentals. Take a good look at Andrew. He was just like you, but he made his life count for his Lord and His cause."

Burleigh Cruikshank

A LOFTIER AMBITION

There is a loftier ambition than merely to stand high in the world. It is to stoop down and lift mankind a little higher. *Henry Van Dyke*

AMERICA NEEDS MEN OF FAITH AND PRAYER

On the courthouse of Cuyahoga County at Cleveland, Ohio, are inscribed these words: "Obedience to Law is Liberty." Recently, one of the judges pointed out that there is a significant omission in the inscription. It comes from Richard Hooker, the 16th Century author and stylist, and what Hooker wrote was this, "Obedience to *Divine* Law is Liberty."

God makes a Bible out of history. It is a Bible that he who runs may read; and that Bible declares that the nation which forgets God shall be cast into Hell. When we have a revival of obedience to Divine Law, then the ramparts which we watch shall be safe. *Clarence Edward Macartney*

PROVIDENTIAL CARE

We use many times the words Providential Care and refer to both the Old and New Testaments to see the Providential Care with which we are surrounded. The ancient Hebrews made this vivid and looked upon Jehovah not only as the God of all Israel but also as the God Who made His ministrations very personal and individual. With this concept in mind, they referred to Him so often as the God of Abraham, Isaac and Jacob.

When we come into the New Testament we see emphasized this individual and personal consideration more and more. Not even the sparrow falls to the ground without His knowing it. "The very hairs of your head are all numbered," "He calleth His own sheep by name," "It is not the will of your Father that one of these little ones should perish." More and more this Providential Care of each one of us was taught and demonstrated as our Lord went into the deeper areas of the revelation of God to man. St. Augustine wrote: "He cares for every one of us as if there were only one of us to care for."

John Robbins Hart

REPENTANCE

Repentance is a hearty sorrow for our past misdeeds, and a sincere resolution and endeavor, to the utmost of our power, to conform all our actions to the law of God. It does not consist in one single act of sorrow, but in doing works meet for repentance; in a sincere obedience to the law of Christ for the remainder of our lives.   *Locke*

TRIUMPHANT FAITH

Someone has said that meeting and defeating evil is the triumph of religion. A traveler says that the first time he heard Hawaiian music he declared that it was tears set to harmony. Only later did he learn that it had been invented by the suffering lepers of Hawaii. The Negro spirituals have had great meaning for us here.

> "Nobody knows the trouble I've seen;
> Nobody knows but Jesus
> Nobody knows the trouble I've seen,
> Glory Halleluiah!"

In the midst of trouble and pain and suffering the "Halleluiah" of Easter breaks forth in glorious victory. Dr. Stanley Jones tells of visiting a leper asylum in the Orient where a Christian worker had caught the dread leprosy himself. All the fingers of his right hand had been eaten off by this horrible disease except the index finger. With that he picked up his violin bow and played beautiful and triumphant music. Instead of going away depressed, Dr. Jones said he went away with a song in his heart for such heroic victory under these evil conditions. If we would put reality into religion let us put away the discouragements and complaints, and let us know an heroic and victorious faith to the world.   *J. Walter Malone*

STEWARDSHIP

We think ourselves masters, when we are only stewards, and forget that to each of us it will one day be said, "Give an account of thy stewardship."   *Bishop Horne*

OUR BURDEN BEARER

The little sharp vexations
  And the briars that cut the feet,
Why not take all to the Helper
  Who has never failed us yet?
Tell him about the heartache,
  And tell him the longings too,
Tell him the baffled purpose
  When we scarce know what to do.
Then, leaving all our weakness
  With the One divinely strong,
Forget that we bore the burden
  And carry away the song.   *Phillips Brooks*

THE BEST IS YET TO BE

Grow Old Along With Me—the best is yet to be. Vanderbilt at 80 added more than a hundred million to his fortune. Wadsworth earned the Laureateship at 73. Thiers at 73 established the French Republic and became the first president. Verdi wrote "Falstaff" at 80. Gladstone became Premier of England for the fourth time at 83. Stradivari made his first violin after 60. And Sir Walter Scott was $600,000 in debt at 55, but through his own efforts paid this amount in full, and built a lasting name for himself.

WE MUST CARRY IT

Though we travel the world over to find the beautiful, we must carry it with us or we find it not.   *Emerson*

THE COLORS I FLEW

For myself, I stand for spiritual life as the interpreter of God and for Jesus Christ as the interpreter of spiritual life. There, I think, is a great credo in a single sentence. I believe in God interpreted in terms of spiritual life and I believe in Jesus Christ as the illustrious revealer of what spiritual life is. In this world with its cynicism, its disillusionment, often its disheartenment, how men and women are needed to stand for that with its intellectual, its personal, and its social implications!

Some flagstaffs are very tall and prominent and some are small, but the glory of a flagstaff is not its size; it is the colors that it flies. A very small flagstaff flying the right colors is far more valuable than a very tall one with the wrong flag. When a man is altogether done with life, I should suppose that the most satisfying thing would be the ability to say, I am ashamed that I was not a better, taller, straighter flagstaff, but I am not ashamed of the colors that I flew.   *Harry Emerson Fosdick*

PRAYER

As a physician, I have seen men, after all other therapy had failed, lifted out of disease and melancholy by the serene effort of prayer.   *Dr. Alexis Carrel*

THE CHURCH

The Church after all is not a club of saints; it is a hospital for sinners.   *George Craig Stewart*

TEACH US TO LOOK ON THEE

Teach us to look in all our ends
On Thee for judge and not our friends;

That we, with Thee, may walk uncowed
By fear or favor of the crowd.   *Rudyard Kipling*

SEND ME

And I heard the voice of the Lord, saying Whom shall I send, and who will go for us? Then I said, Here am I; send me.

Isaiah VI

GENIUS

Genius is commonly developed in men by some deficiency that stabs them wide awake and becomes a major incentive. Obstacles can be immensely arousing and kindling.

Harry Emerson Fosdick

FAITH

Look at the birds of the air: they neither sow nor reap, nor gather into barns; and yet your heavenly Father feeds them. Are you not of more value than they?   *Matthew VI*

THE ONLY SON

And the word became flesh and dwelt among us, full of grace and truth; we have beheld his glory; glory as of the only Son from the Father. No man has ever seen God; the only Son has made him known.   *John I*

THE FATHER

Philip said unto him, "Lord, show us the Father and we shall be satisfied." Jesus said unto him, "Have I been with you so long, and yet you do not know me Philip? He who has seen me has seen the Father."   *John XIV*

UPON HIS CROSS

What a relief if one could conscientiously wash one's hands of the whole concern! But then there is that Strange Man upon his cross who drives one back again and again.

George Tyrrell

LOVE

Only through love can we attain to communion with God.

Dr. Albert Schweitzer

THE CROSS

When I survey the wondrous cross
  On which the Prince of Glory died,
My richest gain I count but loss,
  And pour contempt on all my pride.

Were the whole realm of nature mine,
  That were a present far too small;
Love so amazing, so divine,
  Demands my soul, my life, my all.

Isaac Watts

NO MAN LIVETH TO HIMSELF

Where I lie down worn out, other men will stand young and fresh, By the steps that I have cut they will climb; by the stairs that I have built they will mount. They will never know the name of the man who made them. At the clumsy work they will laugh; when the stones roll they will curse me. But they will mount, and on my work; they will climb, and by my stair! . . . And no man liveth to himself, and no man dieth to himself!   *Oliver Schreiner in Worship Resources for Youth*

THE COMMON PEOPLE

Long live also the forward march of the common people in all the lands towards their just and true inheritance, and toward the broader and fuller age.   *Winston Churchill*

WAR

. . . never think that war, no matter how necessary, nor how justified, is not a crime. Ask the infantry and ask the dead.
Ernest Hemingway

LEAD KINDLY LIGHT

Lead kindly Light, amid th' encircling gloom,
Lead Thou me on;
The night is dark, and I am far from home;
Lead Thou me on:
Keep Thou my feet;
I do not ask to see
The distant scene—one step enough for me.

John H. Newman

DOING THE WILL OF THE FATHER

Enter by the narrow gate; for the gate is wide and the way is easy, that leads to destruction, and those who enter by it are many. For the gate is narrow and the way is hard, that leads to life, and those who find it are few.

Beware of false prophets, who come to you in sheep's clothing but inwardly are ravenous wolves. You will know them by their fruits. Are grapes gathered from thorns, or figs from thistles? So, every sound tree bears good fruit, but the bad tree bears evil fruit. A sound tree cannot bear evil fruit, nor can a bad tree bear good fruit. Every tree that does not bear good fruit is cut down and thrown into the fire. Thus you will know them by their fruits.

Not every one who says to me, Lord, Lord, shall enter the kingdom of heaven, but he who does the will of my Father who is in heaven.   *Matthew VII*

FAITH

One's Faith in God increases as one's faith in the world decreases.   *George Jean Nathan*

COUNTING TIME

We live in deeds, not years; in thoughts, not breaths;
In feelings, not in fingers on a dial.
We should count time by heart-throbs. He most lives
Who thinks most, feels the noblest, acts the best.

                                        P. J. Bailey

HOW LITTLE WE NEED

Half the confusion in the world comes from not knowing how little we need. . . . I live more simply now, and with more peace.   *Admiral Richard E. Byrd*

LOVE

Talk not of wasted affection, affection never was wasted,
If it enrich not the heart of another, its waters, returning
Back to their springs, like the rain, shall fill them full of refreshment;
That which the fountain sends forth returns again to the fountain.   *Henry Wadsworth Longfellow*

MARRIAGE

The highest happiness on earth is in marriage. Every man who is happily married is a successful man even if he has failed in everything else.   *William Lyon Phelps*

LIFE

Nature gives to every time and season some beauties of its own; and from morning to night, as from the cradle to the grave, is but a succession of changes so gentle and easy that we can scarcely mark their progress.   *Charles Dickens*

OLD AGE

As for old age, embrace and love it. It abounds with pleasure if you know how to use it. The gradually declining years are among the sweetest in a man's life; and I maintain that even when they have reached the extreme limit, they have their pleasure still.   *Seneca*

YOU WILL NOT BE TOO BUSY

My friend, there will come one day to you a Messenger, whom you cannot treat with contempt. He will say, "Come with me;" and all your pleas of business cares and earthly loves will be of no avail. When his cold hand touches yours, the key of the counting-room will drop forever, and he will lead you away from all your investments, your speculations, your bank-notes and real estate, and with him you will pass into eternity up to the bar of God. You will not be too busy to die.

A. E. Kittredge

A CHANCE

My country owes me nothing. It gave me, as it gives every boy and girl, a chance. It gave me schooling, independence of action, opportunity for service and honor. In no other land could a boy from a little country village, without inheritance or influential friends, look forward with unbounded hope.

Herbert Hoover

FORGIVENESS

There is no revenge so complete as forgiveness.

H. W. Shaw

FORGIVE OTHERS MUCH

If thou wouldst find much favor and peace with God and man, be very low in thine own eyes. Forgive thyself little, and others much. *Leighton*

GIVING THANKS

Lord God of Hosts, be with us yet,
Lest we forget—lest we forget! *Kipling*

FOR ME TO LIVE IN CHRIST

I entreat you to devote one solemn hour of thought to a crucified Saviour—a Saviour expiring in the bitterest agony. Think of the cross, the nails, the open wounds, the anguish of His soul. Think how the Son of God became a man of sorrows and acquainted with grief, that you might live forever. Think as you lie down upon your bed to rest, how your Saviour was lifted up from the earth to die. Think amid your plans and anticipations of future gaiety what the redemption of your soul has cost, and how the dying Saviour would wish you to act. His wounds plead that you will live for better things.

Albert Barnes

NOT WITHOUT CHRIST

A man may go to heaven without health, without riches, without honors, without learning, without friends, but he can never go there without Christ. *John Dyer*

THE CHURCH

Jesus organized the church, which is His vineyard. He commands all to go into the vineyard and work. All who are united to Christ by faith, and are thus members of His mystical body, should be members of His visible church.   *Aughey*

FOR THE WEARY AND TROUBLED

The church is not a select circle of the immaculate, but a home where the outcast may come in. It is not a palace with gate attendants and challenging sentinels along the entrance-ways holding off at arm's length the stranger, but rather a hospital where the broken-hearted may be healed, and where all the weary and troubled may find rest and take counsel together.   *Aughey*

THE AMERICAN NATION

Our nation was founded as an experiment in human liberty. Its institutions reflected the belief of our founders that men had their origin and destiny in God; that they were endowed by Him with certain inalienable rights and had duties prescribed by moral law; and that human institutions ought primarily to help men develop their God-given possibilities. We believed that if we built on that spiritual foundation we would be showing men everywhere the way to a better and more abundant life.

We realized that vision. There developed here an area of spiritual, intellectual and economic vigor, the like of which the world had never seen. It was no exclusive preserve; indeed world mission was a central theme. Millions were welcomed from other lands, to share equally the opportunities of the founders and their heirs. Through missionary activities, the establishment of schools and colleges and through travel, American ideals were carried throughout the world. We gave

aid and comfort to those elsewhere who sought to follow in
our way and to develop societies of greater freedom.

John Foster Dulles

COME UNTO ME

I have read in Plato and Cicero sayings that are very wise
and very beautiful; but I never read in either of them, "Come
unto me, all ye that labor and are heavy laden."

St. Augustine

FOUNDED UPON LOVE

Alexander, Caesar, Charlemagne and I myself have founded
empires; but upon what do these creations of our genius depend? Upon force. Jesus alone founded His empire upon love:
and to this very day millions would die for him.

Napoleon I

LIFE IS AN ALTAR

Too many believe life is a crib from which they are privileged to feed. Out of it they demand clothing and food and
money and power. That isn't living at all. Life is an altar,
and the things that go on altars are sacrifices.

Preston Bradley

LIVE IS NOT AT FAULT

One man gets nothing but discord out of a piano; another
gets harmony. No one claims the piano is at fault. Life is
about the same. The discord is there, and the harmony is
there. Study to play it correctly, and it will give forth the
beauty; play it falsely, and it will give forth the ugliness.
Life is not at fault.   *Sunshine Magazine*

MERCY

We hand folks over to God's mercy, and show none our-selves. *George Eliot*

PEACE

The world will never have lasting peace so long as men reserve for war the finest human qualities. Peace, no less than war, requires idealism and self-sacrifice and a righteous and dynamic faith. *John Foster Dulles*

CHRIST EVERYWHERE

The results of splitting the world into secular and sacred sections have become disastrous. We have fenced off a nice little area of life and labeled it religion. That is not enough. We must take Christ into our factories, schools, newspaper officers, businesses, homes, everywhere.

Thomas N. Carruthers

A GREAT WORK

Never before has so large a percentage of this nation be-longed to the Chruch. Never before have so many people around the world belonged to the Church. The Church out-numbers every empire on earth. Jesus Christ has more con-fessed followers than any modern head of state. We have enough man power to do anything which needs to be done in the world.

We have the people. Everything depends upon whether or not the people will have a mind to work.

We must work with wisdom. The tasks of Jesus Christ deserve our best intelligence. We must work with faith, con-tent to do our best and trust God with the rest . . . Someone has told of a little girl who fell out of bed. She explained the accident later by saying: "I guess I went to sleep too close to the place where I got in." If only so many of us in the Church would not go "to sleep too close to the place where we got in."

To do a great work we must work: work with wisdom, with faith, with harmony, and above all, work!

Everett W. Palmer

QUIETNESS IN LIFE

Have you ever felt that life was all tangled up and you couldn't find the way out? Then did you ever go and sit beside a lake or stream just as the stars came out? All was calm and peaceful. Somehow a quietness had come to you, and you felt capable of facing life again.

THE PAST

Look not mournfully into the past; it comes not back. Wisely improve the present. *Longfellow*

TROUBLE

We should never attempt to bear more than one kind of trouble at a time. Some people try to bear three kinds—all they have had, all they have now, and all they expect to have.

Edward Everett Hale

THE DIFFERENCE

A leading actor was honored at a banquet. In the after-dinner ceremonies the actor was asked to recite for the pleasure of his guests. He consented, and asked if there was anything special anyone in the audience would like to hear.

There was a moment's pause, and then an old clergyman spoke up. "Could you, sir," he said, "recite the twenty-third Psalm?"

A strange look came over the actor's face, but he was speechless for only a moment. "I can, sir—and I will, on one condition, and that is that after I have recited, you, my friend, will do the same."

"I?" replied the surprised clergyman; "but I am not an elocutionist. However, if you wish, I will do so."

Impressively the great actor began the Psalm, holding his audience spellbound. As he finished, a great burst of applause broke from the guests.

After the applause had ceased, the old clergyman arose. The audience sat in intense silence. The Psalm was recited, and when it was done, there was not the slightest ripple of applause, but those in the audience whose eyes were yet dry had their heads bowed.

The great actor, with hand on the shoulder of the old clergyman, his voice trembling, exclaimed, "I reached your eyes and ears, my friends, this man reached your hearts; I know the twenty-third Psalm, this man knows the Shepherd."

ACCOMPLISHMENT

Nearly two-thirds of all the greatest deeds ever performed by human beings—the victories in battle, the greatest books, the greatest pictures and statues—have been accomplished after the age of sixty. *Albert Edward Wiggam*

NEVER TOO LATE TO ACHIEVE

At about the age when many men begin to consider themselves crossing over to the shady side of life—the half-century mark—Sir Christopher Wren, who built magnificent St. Paul's Cathedral in London in the seventeenth century, was entering enthusiastically upon a new career in a new profession. After serving as professor of astronomy at Gresham College and Oxford, he turned architect.

In the forty-one years after his forty-eighth birthday this amazing man executed fifty-three churches and cathedrals, most of which still stand as monuments to his greatness.

Robert R. Updegraff

PRIVATE CHARITY

The day we decide that the government is our brother's keeper, that day the spirit of compassion will have been lost. If we abandon private charity, we will have lost something to America's material, moral, and spiritual welfare.

Herbert Hoover

CHRISTMAS

I have always thought of Christmas time when it has come round, as a good time; a kind, forgiving, charitable time; the only time I know, in the long calendar of the year, when men and women seem by one consent to open their shut-up hearts freely, and to think of people below them as if they really were fellow passengers to the grave, and not another race of creatures bound on other journeys.   *Charles Dickens*

HOW OUR NATION WAS BUILT

Our nation was built by men who took risks—pioneers who were not afraid of the wilderness; brave men who were not afraid of failure; scientists who were not afraid of truth; thinkers who were not afraid of progress; dreamers who were not afraid of action.   *Brooks Atkinson*

EASTER DAY

Something happened on Easter Day which made Christ more alive on the streets of Jerusalem forty days after his crucifixion than on the day of His Triumphal Entry. A false report might last forty days but the church which was founded on a Risen Christ has lasted for nineteen centuries, producing generations of the race's finest characters and now including some six hundred million members.   *Ralph W. Sockman*

FORGIVENESS

Doing an injury puts you below your enemy; revenging one makes you even with him; forgiving it sets you above him.

Nylic Review

CHRISTMAS SHOPPING

Few people ever put Christ on their "shopping list." In all the vast crowds, not one in ten thousand is looking for a present to give to the Christ child. His name never appears on these long secret lists along with Aunt Sarah and Cousin Joe . . . no gift on sale at any store would be suitable. Tragically, the far greater truth is that most of us never think of making a Christmas gift to Christ.

Halford E. Luccock and Robert E. Luccock

BROTHERHOOD

We are no nearer to God than we are to the person or group of human beings for whom we care the least.

SELF-RIGHTEOUS

The hardest people to reach with the love of God are not the bad people. They know they are bad. They have no defense. The hardest ones to win for God are the self-righteous people. *Charles L. Allen*

YOUR HANDICAPS

If you have the idea that physical perfection is necessary to success in your chosen field, take a look at this even dozen of famous men and the handicaps that failed to slow them: Lord Byron had a clubfoot; Robert Louis Stevenson and John Keats had tuberculosis. Charles Steinmetz and Alexander Pope

were hunchbacks; Admiral Nelson had only one eye; Edgar
Allan Poe was a psycho-neurotic; Charles Darwin was an in-
valid; Julius Caesar was an epileptic; Thomas Edison and
Ludwig von Beethoven were deaf, and Peter Stuyvesant had
a wooden leg.   *Wilfred Funk*

NO OTHER SOLUTION

You may think that I am ultra-idealistic. You may be cynical
and may scoff. But we can have charters, and we can have
conferences; we can go through all the maneuvers and theories,
but only one thing can assure enduring peace. There is no
solution save the rule of Christ alone. Religion is the only
thing that will do it. The love of man for man.

Senator Charles William Tobey

SEEK FIRST THE KINGDOM OF GOD

Jesus pointed out that, in his time, the nations of the world
were giving priority to material things. He called upon men
to seek first the Kingdom of God. Material things would then
be added unto them. But such things would be a by-product,
not a primary goal.

It is of the greatest importance to bear that distinction in
mind as we face the challenge of an atheistic society which
avowedly puts first the search for material things. . . .

We must *not* accept an armaments race, as if to be the
greatest military power were a worthy or even acceptable goal.

We must *not* seek that scientific education and scientific
applications monopolize the minds of our youth, as though
other values did not matter.

We must *not* accept the quantity of consumer's goods—
automobiles, washing machines, refrigerators, radios, and the
like—to be the decisive measure of our society, as though its
spiritual content were unimportant.   *John Foster Dulles*

TRIALS

There will be no Christian but will have a Gethsemane; but every praying Christian will find that there is no Gethsemane without its angel!   *T. Binney*

INDEX

A

Able, 89
Accomplishment, 113
Affliction, 89
Age, 37, 41, 88, 90, 101, 107, 113
Alone, 88
Ambition, 24, 99
America, 38, 109, 114
Anger, 90
Anxious, 70
Atonement, 32

B

Bargains, 23
Beauty, 38
Beggar, 53
Begin Now, 54
Bell, 45
Benedictions, 61
Bible, 9, 91, 99
Bread, 28
Brotherhood, 115
Burden, 79, 101

C

Care, 99
Challenge, 83
Chance, 38, 107
Character, 14, 25, 48
Charity, 18, 26, 40, 41, 114
Children, 47, 49, 58, 65, 94
Christ, 87, 108
Christianity, 28
Christmas, 28, 29, 89, 114
Christmas Shopping, 115
Church, 29, 49, 102, 109, 111
Comfort, 52
Common People, 105
Communion, 65

Conscience, 41, 58, 85
Contentment, 72
Conversion, 46
Cornerstone, 64
Country, 80
Courage, 10, 25, 56, 59
Cross, 64, 104
Crowd, 102

D

Death, 16, 30, 42, 62, 64, 75, 76, 107
Decision, 23
Desperation, 58
Despair, 77
Deeds, 82
Dreams, 16, 66, 69
Duty, 39

E

Ease, 35
Easter, 30, 114
Enemies, 82
Experience, 38

F

Failure, 21
Fairy Tale, 35
Faith, 52, 59, 74, 94, 100, 103, 106
Fame, 10, 30
Family, 66, 79
Father, 86, 103
Fear, 26, 55
Fool, 39, 42
Forgiveness, 12, 57, 65, 78, 82, 108, 115
Fortress, 42

G

Genius, 103
Giving, 62, 84

119

Glory, 25
God, 33, 36, 44, 55, 60, 68, 71, 76, 83, 88
Good, 77, 82
Good Name, 36
Good-night, 60
Good Will, 19, 29
Good Works, 39
Gossip, 67
Greatness, 10
Grief, 48, 62, 75

H

Handicaps, 60, 115
Happiness, 22, 71, 72
Hardship, 90
Heart, 17, 113
Hearthstone, 91
Help, 39, 49, 69, 77
Hill, 41
History, 28
Holy Ground, 32
Home, 35, 43
Hope, 54, 80
Hour, 43
Human Affairs, 79
Humility, 96, 97

I

Ignorance, 40
Immortality, 34, 43, 55
Inspiration, 86, 94

K

Kind Deed, 16
Kindness, 27, 33, 45, 96
Kingdom, 116
Knowledge, 35, 36

L

Lepers, 44
Liberty, 20
Life, 13, 17, 18, 20, 30, 45, 47, 60, 73, 78, 97, 107, 110
Light, 105
Lilies, 69
Look Ahead, 14

Lord, 51
Love, 17, 36, 48, 65, 68, 95, 104, 106, 110

M

Man, 66, 70
Memories, 40, 67
Men, 22, 23, 35
Men of God, 13
Mercy, 51, 52, 68, 111
Mistake, 77
Modesty, 21
Money, 47, 64, 73, 85
Monuments, 36
Mother, 11, 69

N

Naturalness, 16
Nature, 57
Need, 48, 106
Neighbor, 42, 71, 94
Noble, 87

O

Objective, 32
Old and New, 14
Once, 35
Ourselves, 38

P

Pain, 51
Parents, 80
Pass It On, 34
Past, 112
Path, 86
Patience, 20, 53
Peace, 41, 55, 80, 83, 85, 111
Perseverance, 77
Pharisee, 57
Poor, 63
Prayer, 57, 60, 71, 75, 80, 102
Progress, 9

Q

Quietness, 112

R

Rain, 56
Religion, 11, 31, 111, 116
Repentance, 100
Respect, 76
Responsibility, 97
Rest, 63, 74
Revenge, 33
Right, 49, 66

S

Sabbath, 13
Sacrifice, 10
Salvation, 12
Satisfied, 10
Scars, 45
Self-Righteous, 115
Sermon, 91
Sharing, 68
Shepherd, 50, 89
Sorrow, 63
Soul, 20
Stars, 73
Stewardship, 101
Strength, 9
Success, 39

T

Task, 70

Tears, 44
Temple, 61
Thanksgiving, 11
Think, 82
Thoughts, 17, 33
Time, 106
Tomorrow, 79
Training, 71
Trials, 117
Trouble, 112
Truth, 88

U

Unhappiness, 73

V

Vice, 54
Vision, 52

W

War, 105
Water, 96
Winter, 70
Wisdom, 10
Women, 22
Wonder, 27
Work, 76
World, 63